SPEAK
Positively

I0082302

GLOBAL
PUBLISHING
G R O U P

Global Publishing Group
Australia • New Zealand • Singapore • America • London

SPEAK *Positively*

Manifest what you
really want
by saying what you
really mean

Foreword by Brandon Bays
– Author of "The Journey"

JAN HENDERSON

First Edition 2020

Copyright © 2020 Jan Henderson

National Library of Australia
Cataloguing-in-Publication entry:

Speak Positively: Manifest what you really want by saying what you really mean - Jan Henderson

1st ed.
ISBN: 978-1-925288-97-1 (pbk.)

A catalogue record for this book is available from the National Library of Australia

Published by Global Publishing Group
PO Box 517 Mt Evelyn, Victoria 3796 Australia
Email Info@GlobalPublishingGroup.com.au

Printed in Australia

For further information about orders:
Phone: +61 3 9726 4133

This book is dedicated to
My two sons, James and Mark,
who have always believed in
their Mum

♡

ACKNOWLEDGEMENTS

There have been so many people who have contributed to getting this book to print. Top of my gratitude list is my brother Paul who has been an enduring tower of strength. He was the first to identify that I was unhappy – when I refused to admit it. In 1991, he presented me with the genesis of this book back when he asked me to retype an Emergency Procedures Manual for a coal mine he was managing. On each of the 200+ pages were the words "Don't Panic!" Needless to say, they were changed to "Stay Calm."

Deep gratitude goes to Brandon Bays and Kevin Billett from The Journey Method. Their programs of self-awareness and self-realisation are profound and life-changing. Kevin's work "Healing with Conscious Communication" and his work on Depression – "Light in the Heart of Darkness", both had a profound effect on me – and changed the way I speak, as well as communicate, and has ultimately given me the courage to write this book. My gratitude also to Brandon for writing the Foreword to this book.

Gratitude also to Wayne and Susie Christiansen who have been so supportive over the years.

Gratitude as well to the people I met during the process of writing this book, particularly Tanya de Haan. We shared many conversations and ideas. Gratitude also to those who have allowed me to share their stories. Some names have been changed at their request, others are direct quotes.

Gratitude also goes to my two beautiful sons, James and Mark. They are an inspiration and make me a very proud parent every day of their lives. Equally, gratitude goes to Dawn – my daughter-in-law. She has been helpful, particularly with information on working with children on the spectrum. As a teacher, she uses positive language with her students every day and knows the impact language has on a child's development.

To my dear granddaughters, Anna, Lauren and Courtney, and to my dear step-grandsons Harvey and Spencer, Australia is in good hands with you all coming through to take the reins. To Shelley, (Harvey and Spencer's mum) your love and support is deeply valued.

To my "support team" – Suzanne and Rhonda – your encouragement and love have sustained me. The phone calls when I need to vent and the opportunity to workshop issues and ideas have been an enormous resource.

To Megan Bardsley and Sharon Kolkka and the team from Gwinganna Lifestyle Retreat at Tallebudgera in Queensland – my deepest gratitude. You change lives every single day of the year. Your love and support are deeply appreciated.

Lastly, to Darren Stephens and his team at Global Publishing Group in Melbourne. Without their help, this book would not have come to fruition.

FREE
BONUS GIFTS

Claim your FREE BONUS GIFTS by going to:

www.JanHenderson.com.au/Book-Bonuses

GIFT LOADING...

Instant Access and Free Download

Make sure you get your FREE tools and create your own Positivity

BONUS #1: FEAR LIST Jan's personally developed list of fears for you to print off and use.

BONUS #2: FEELING WORDS At a loss to describe how you are feeling? Print this list and check it to help you identify the feeling.

BONUS #3: eBOOK – The Journey by Brandon Bays Access the book that changed Jan's life by International Bestselling Author. More than 5 million copies sold.

www.JanHenderson.com.au/Book-Bonuses

CONTENTS

FOREWORD

Jan is a living example of recognising and listening intently to a deeper knowing, a knowing that we all possess often buried under the debris of our life experiences, traumas, choices and shut downs. In the face of life's trials and setbacks she held on to the light that is in all of us. Through self-reflection and introspection she made the choice to 'stop the story' and hence transformed her life, and found her way back home to the truth of her own being.

Her honest exposure of the pain created by unconscious communication, disempowering beliefs, family expectations and looking outwards for her sense of self invites you, the reader, to do the same.

Through her own personal stories and experiences of letting go of the lies she was told, the beliefs that were ingrained in her and the incongruent expectations placed upon her, she opens us all into the possibility of true freedom, conscious choice and living life in clear awareness.

Jan guides you on a journey of deep inner listening, encouraging you to drop the false meanings you have attached to your repetitive mind talk and pay attention to your natural emotions. In doing so, she offers the greatest gift: the gift of being reunited with yourself; with that innocent, shining and free soul that is your essence.

Jan's unwavering determination and deep insights inspire us all to live life freshly in each moment and remain vigilant to the strategies we use to hide our light. She encourages us to flourish our sense of meaning and purpose in life, and to love deeply as shining examples of infinite presence.

Brandon Bays
Founder of The Journey Method and Internationally Best Selling Author of The Journey, Freedom Is, Living the Journey, and Light in the Heart of Darkness

A NOTE FROM JAN

♡

This book had its genesis back in 1991 when my brother Paul asked me to retype the emergency procedures manual for a coal mine. He was the general manager, and it was a vital task he had to fulfil.

There were pages and pages in the old manual, and on the top of each page were the words "Don't Panic!" They were typed in RED, so they stood out. You could say they "screamed" at me. It was total disbelief that there was an official manual that used such profoundly negative words. The instruction was actually saying, "PANIC." The manual was subsequently updated, and on the top of each page when it left my office were the words "STAY CALM."

In the ensuing years, little messages such as these have entered my awareness. I have run self-awareness courses and have workshopped negative language.

Late last year, I was binge-watching a TV series and was astounded at the number of negative phrases used – to the point I began writing them down, not really sure what I was going to do with them. The plan at the time was to add them to my growing list and develop a further workshop. The idea of putting together a book evolved. If these words change your life, then I have further fulfilled my mission for this life.

Enjoy reading.

CHAPTER 1

Introduction

♡

What you think, and what you feel ...
and what manifests is always a match.
Every single time. No exceptions.

Esther Hicks

CHAPTER 1

Introduction

For so long, I heard those words, and yet they never really "clicked." I read so many books and took so many courses. I tried affirmations, and they worked for a limited time. I tried them all. I listened to the promises. I read the secret behind "the secret" – that there is a magic way to manifest the love of your life; the car of your dreams, how to win the lottery – how to "have it all." The manifesting gurus insist there is a specific way to visualise, to meditate, to dream, to stand, to use affirmations, to use music, etc., etc., etc. On and on it goes. There are thousands of books, tapes, CDs, and techniques available, some of which are magnificent and most of which work – temporarily.

This book is going to try to give you some clues about why all those wonderful techniques you tried – and which may have worked for you in the beginning – are forgotten when you get back into "normal" life so you are back to where you began. All of them have failed you, and they will continue to fail you because what they forget to mention is the underlying silent hackers that plague us all. These silent hackers are quietly playing havoc in our lives.

Silent Hackers

One of those silent hackers is the language we use. We have been taught to speak negatively. Yes, from the very beginning of our

www.JanHenderson.com.au

lives, one of the first words we hear is "No!" Then, the next thing we become aware of is "don't do this" "don't do that." It is in our everyday language. We say the words every minute of every day without appreciating what we are saying. We never hear what we are saying. You receive an email, see advertising, or a sign which implores you to "don't miss" this; or "you don't want to miss" that; "don't forget such and such" or "don't park here."

All of this language is spoken or written unconsciously. Have you ever stopped to consider what these messages are really saying to you, and more importantly, how you "hear" them? Do you realise how much power is contained in the words you write and say? Have you ever stopped to consider the power of the thoughts you think and how the words you speak impact yourself as well as others?

In my life, I have become acutely aware of the impact of the words which come out of my mouth and those I write. I have become conscious of the thoughts I am thinking. In the past, I was unconscious, walking around speaking and saying things which I expected people to understand, and was surprised when I got a completely different reaction to the one expected or more commonly blank looks of bewilderment.

Recently, I have been working with a 13-year-old who is considered "on the spectrum."[1] He is an absolute delight to speak with, and we connected when I showed him the following sign.

---

1. Autism is a neurodevelopmental disability that affects the way people communicate and interact with the world. Characteristics generally appear in early childhood and will be present, in some form, for life. Taken from www.amaze.org.au Shaping the future for Autism.

Photo: Woolworths Chirnside Park, Victoria

He was immediately able to identify the mixed messages displayed. One is a positive message "Please return your trolley here"; the other one is confusing – does it mean "remember to take your bags INTO the supermarket" or "remember to take your bags out of the trolley?"

People "on the spectrum" read this sign literally. They read the words "park your trolley here" and "forget" your bags. They are unable to process the negative word "don't." They will process the word "forget" before they process anything else.

An interesting example on the subject of working with children on the spectrum occurred for my daughter-in-law, who is a Grade 2 teacher. She had a young child at school who was removed from the classroom because he was disruptive. Another teacher took the child to her office and said the child could play with a ball, as a means to distract and calm him. The child heard the words "you can play with the ball" to mean he can play with the ball in the hallway as well as in the teacher's office; in fact, he can play with the ball anywhere he likes. He could not comprehend that he should only play with the ball in the teacher's office, because that was not what she said. He took her literally when she said, "you can play with the ball." If the teacher's aim was to calm the child, it would have been better for the child to be taken to the sensory room so he could calm himself by reading or listening to music.

What is the *real* intent of your communication? When you speak, are you speaking consciously? What are you manifesting by the words you are saying and the thoughts you are thinking? Are you like the teacher above who told the child to "play with the ball" when she meant for him to play quietly with the ball in her office?

Just for a moment, remember the words your mother or father said to you as a child. "It's not your turn to speak"; "don't cross the road"; "don't run"; "children should be seen and not heard"; "don't make a mess with your ice cream"; "don't be nervous"; "you'll get hurt if you do that"; "don't leave the lights on"; "don't be afraid"; "don't cry"; "don't get out of bed"; "don't move"; "don't forget" "don't bother me right now". How have those words affected you?

How did the words your teachers spoke influenced the way you learn? "You are no good"; "you are a lazy good for nothing, useless son of a b****"; "don't slam the door"; don't listen to your negative talk"; "there's not a creative bone in your body"; "you're a loser"; "you'll never be successful"; "you'll never amount to anything"; "you're no good at…"

How have the words your siblings said to you affected the way you react to them and to life? "You're just a mistake"; "you're a loser"; "you're a dummy"; "you're just a moron."

How have all of these statements governed the way you deal with life? How have the words written in a text message damaged a relationship? How have the words spoken by a partner affected your self-esteem?

Words impact our lives every minute of every day. They have the power to lift us up or knock us down. They have the power to make us feel good or bad; they can boost our self-esteem or cause us to wallow in self-hatred. They have the power to elevate our belief in ourselves or to deplete the very fabric of our existence. There is a whole chapter following on **The Secrets to Self-Esteem over Self-Harm**.

The more we become conscious of the language we use, the more we understand the full force of those words. Have you heard people say "this is killing me?" Or what about "that drives me crazy," or even worse, "this drives me insane?" I have caught myself being astounded at things a friend does and saying "You are insane", or "You are crazy". I now hear these words as criticism. There is an epidemic of Alzheimer's and dementia in the world today. Is it possible that these diseases have been self-manifested? It is impossible, of course, for me to say, as I am not aware of any definitive research into language and disease, but it would be an interesting PhD. subject. In the chapter **How What You Say Manifests Health or Disease**, the aspect of language on health is examined a little further.

Unfortunately, most of us have no idea we are speaking in the negative. We, therefore, fail to realise how much this impacts our lives. We are limiting ourselves and each other.

When we say words such as "don't be surprised," what do we really mean? Am I supposed to be surprised, or astonished, or am I supposed to expect something... as in "don't be surprised when I..."

When you say "don't slam the door," do you mean "please close the door quietly?" What about "don't talk so loudly?" Do you mean "can you please talk softly?" Does "don't make a mess in the kitchen" really mean "if you prepare something in the kitchen, can you please clean up after yourself" or "please leave the kitchen clean?" Does "don't be afraid" really mean "you may experience a little fear, and just know that you are safe?" Or does it mean "I'm concerned about you?"

What about "I can't tell you how excited I am?" Could it translate to "I am excited to be here" or "I want to tell you how pleased and thrilled I am to be here?"

A really good one I heard recently is "they're not bad people!" Are we so afraid to say someone is a nice or a good person? What about "not a bad place for lunch" Again, is it so difficult to say "it's a great place to eat?" One of my favourites is "it's not cheap" when we are trying to say it costs a lot of money.

Why is it so challenging for us to speak in the positive? Why, when we are expressing grief, are we unable to say "We are so proud of him/her" instead we say "He never ceased to make us proud". I'm sure the people in this case, were trying to express their pride in their loved one, and it came across in such a convoluted way. A lot more of these examples are covered in the chapter **How to be a HERO, Not a Victim.**

An entire Universe exists in every word you say.

Words have power. We "give our word" as a way of sealing a bond or agreement. We "give our word" as a treaty between combatants, between nations and people. We "give our word" in the form of a handshake. We "give our word" in the form of an oath – in a court of law, we affirm we will tell the truth, or in marriage or commitment ceremonies, we affirm we will honour our life partner by being true to them alone. We "give our word" when we share intimate details with another. We "give our word" in a simple nod in acknowledgment of another's circumstances.

Breaking our word shatters commitment. Breaking our word devastates a relationship or a person. Breaking our word brings feelings of betrayal. Breaking our word severs a bond of trust between two people, between an employer and an employee, between a government and its people, between allies. Breaking our word can cause a "world war" – between nations, cultures, or individuals.

Speaking words of resentment, anger, hate or judgment causes distress, disharmony, disassociation and disunity. Your words make a difference, as we will see in the chapters **How to be a Leader Instead of a Follower,** and **How Truth is More Powerful than Lies.**

Words and thoughts are the creative tools through which we form stories. These stories form our lives. They can be in the written form in texts, emails, letters or books, or in the spoken stories handed down through generations. Our indigenous ancestors handed down history through stories.

There are magical words written in poetry which express boundless joy and happiness, or profound sadness or despair. There are words of inspiration. There are words of love, devotion and dedication. There are words of anger, hate and revenge, and judgment, words of jealousy, bitterness, or words that make no sense whatsoever. Some words can put us down or some words make our hearts sing.

We have our own stories that we create every day. They are the thoughts we tell ourselves about a look from a loved one, a tone of voice and inflection; a dismissal – these stories influence everything. They influence how we stand, how we walk, how we speak, how we interact with ourselves and others. Most of these stories are made up. They are figments of our imagination. They are an illusion. We hallucinate when we assume a meaning about something said. These illusions and hallucinations can be very damaging to us and our relationships. Depending on our personality, they can play over and over in our heads and cause us to go into panic, anxiety and turmoil. They also can manifest the lives in which we are living.

Words spoken to us – whether they be in the form of simple statements such as "you will never amount to anything" have profound imprints on our being. The story of "I'm not good enough" or "I'll never be enough" play out, not only when we are children, they also play out if we are the cleaner or the CEO of a large corporation or if we are the leader of the free world, responsible for creating peace or war.

Consider, for example, if you removed the word "deserve" from your internal dictionary; how would that change your life? For some people, deleting that one word from their vocabulary has enough power to alter their finances. You may think that is an exaggeration. Think about having a conversation with someone who continually tells themselves that they *deserve* to buy something because they had a bad day or a good day; they *deserve* to have a drink because they have experienced a stressful situation; they *deserve* to have a holiday because they haven't been away from home or the office for a month. This *"deserving"* is a reward system. It is an expensive habit that can have serious consequences for your bank balance and credit cards.

How would it feel if you could *choose* to purchase something "just because" or you could *choose* to have a drink "just because?" You could *choose* to have a holiday "just because." No need to justify anything. Stop for a moment and try out both scenarios – and see how you feel in your body. What is the difference? See how you feel when you choose to remove the word "deserve." Can you appreciate the word *deserve* represents a negative consciousness?

Let's consider another consequence. Words can make or break. They can even kill. You have decided to end friendships because of a word someone used. You have decided whether you will or will not speak with someone because of a word they used. How many times have you decided that "they" should call me first; or that "they" used THAT word; each of us has made up a list

of words that people cannot say to us. If they use THAT word, then they have crossed the line. You probably have kept the list to yourself. No one else knows the rules by which you live. Not only have you decided on the list (which you constantly add to), you also add music to it!! Yes, the music is the tone in which people say the words on the list. Then you add the volume and story.

Do you have rule books? You know, the one that says you (meaning a partner or close friend) MUST do this, or you MUST do that? Does everyone understand your rules? And what happens when they don't? How do you feel? I wasn't aware, until recently, that I was living by someone else's rules!!! I wasn't allowed to be emotional (when I am a very emotional person). So, with what rules do you live? Were you raised in a family that had strict rules – and are these governing your life even now? Who told you, you weren't allowed to do something? Who told you, you weren't good enough? The list is endless. All of my life I have lived by the rule that I was not allowed to be successful. This whole subject of rules is discussed further in the chapter **The Keys to Success over Failure**.

A commonly discussed subject in recent times is the prevalence of misrepresentation of the truth. Take, for example, the phenomena of catfishing. A "catfish" is slang for someone who seduces a person online with a false identity. The advent of social media has introduced a whole new way people can communicate. It isn't necessary to talk to each other either face to face or by phone. Even if a phone conversation occurs, the catfish knows how to avoid being seen by sending text messages or emails so they can hide their true selves. This subject of lying is extensively covered in the chapter on **How Truth is More Powerful than Lies**.

> *The happiness of your life depends upon the quality of your thoughts ... Take care that you entertain no notions unsuitable to virtue and reasonable nature.*
>
> Marcus Aurelius

This quote, from Marcus Aurelius, recognises the power of words and right speech as fundamental teaching in the ancient Greek mystery schools, where the academics and enlightened ones went to learn. These skills are essential to anyone striving to master a successful and empowered life.

It isn't necessary to go to a mystery school to learn how to use words to their full and positive advantage. You can learn those skills right here. Right now. You can learn to remove negative words and replace them with positive ones. You can learn instead of saying, "please don't do that" you can say, "can you please do…?" Instead of saying "don't leave the lights on," you can say, "can you please turn the lights off?" Instead of saying, "you're not wrong," how nice is it to say, "you're right!" The whole energy around all of these changes what is being said, and more importantly, what is being heard.

Yes, it is as simple as that. We have been taught to speak in the negative. We are asking for the very thing we do not want, instead of asking for what we really want and need. When you carefully choose your self-talk, when you carefully select the words you speak to others, when you are mindful of the words you use to interpret the experiences of your life, then the quality of your

life, your health and your relationships will change. The very essence of what it means to become a conscious person begins with examining the content of your vocabulary and its power to shape, define and order your inner and outer Universe. Then you can truly say **Love conquers Hate.**

The subject of this book is to explore the power of the words you use and the power of your thoughts to get a result, to get what you really want. "WHAT IS THE POSITIVE INTENT OF YOUR COMMUNICATION?"

CHAPTER 2

The Keys To Success Over Failure

♡

You aren't allowed to be successful.
You can be the power behind the throne –
you can't sit on it.

My mum

CHAPTER 2

The Keys to Success Over Failure

One of my clients asked me, "How did you get where you are today?" In response, I said, "I was hungry." Hunger is an amazing motivator. When I am hungry, I will do anything it takes to get sustenance.

For centuries, people have been migrating all over the world for the promise of a better life – the promise of success. They risk everything, even their lives. They are hungry. Hunger, in this case, is not for food. It is deeper than that – it is a yearning for something more – for achievement.

As I am writing this, the bodies of 39 people have been located in a truck in the United Kingdom. They were illegal migrants, mostly from Vietnam, attempting to get to what they perceived to be a better life in a more affluent country. Their families paid large sums of money to get them passage – all for the promise of a better life.

When I was growing up, Darling Harbour in Sydney, was a place I was not allowed to visit. I was forbidden to go there. It was a female free zone. I can still hear the words being said, decades

20

later. My breath shortens, my chest tightens, I feel a constriction in my lungs – I have chosen to take deep breaths consciously. The memories are still here. I'm sitting, closing my eyes to keep my focus on what it is I am feeling. Breathing deeply, there is a tightness in my left arm. Is this anxiety, or is it something else? I cough, and I remember that so often when I am experiencing a strong emotion, I cough. What is it I'm feeling? I take my time as I know that I have buried my emotions around this issue so deep, that it takes time for them to arise.

Darling Harbour was the original port area of Sydney. It was here that goods were imported and exported, loaded and unloaded from ships, railway wagons, and road trucks. It was a conglomeration of railway tracks, roads and goods sheds, and a portion of it was known as the Railway Goods Yard. In the 1950s, 60s, and 70s, it was a dark, dirty, dingy, male-only environment. The ground was black from the coal transported to the ships. It was also a dangerous place.

The history of the harbour has been embodied in the ships which used it, the shipyards and wharves along its shores, and the myriad of factories and warehouses that grew up in the surrounding streets. The Market Street Wharf (where Sydney Aquarium now stands) was built in the 1820s and is the only remaining wharf from this era.

For much of the nineteenth century, wheat, wool, coal and timber were the principal cargoes to pass across the wharves but from the 1870s wool became the prime commodity. In 1855 the railway line that ran from the old Central Station was built as part of the first line in New South Wales. A major railway goods yard was established on the Ultimo side of the harbour in the 1870s. In 1874, the world's first full iron wharf was built where Tumbalong Park now stands. The Iron Wharf was considered one of the great engineering feats of the time and was the largest steel structure in the world until the construction of the Eiffel Tower.

Extract from https://darlingharbour.com/learn-explore/history-and-heritage/

Into this environment, enter my father. In the early 1950s he went to Sydney to establish a transport hub to carry kegs of beer, cartons of wine and spirits as well as other general freight destined for the North Coast. My grandfather, dad and uncle had a freight rail business, which they operated out of C Shed, and they held one of the few wholesale liquor licences for the Northern Rivers area of New South Wales. The railway goods wagons would be loaded and packed to the brim ready at a certain time, to be coupled to other goods wagons ready for the engine to leave Darling Harbour on the journey north to Brisbane.

The following is a photo of a restored goods carriage used to transport Arnott's biscuits – it is copied from the Oberon Tarana Heritage Railway Inc website (http://othr.com.au/) – which in turn was copied from ttp://www.nswrollingstock.com/ABV.htm.

It is a visual example of the type of goods wagon I remember being used in Darling Harbour.

Growing up, my father drank alcohol each night (he purchased his favourite Johnny Walker scotch not by the bottle or the box, but by the pallet!). When I was young, he was very angry, and my siblings and I bore the brunt of some of that anger. He and my mother had six children under the age of eight, so the stresses and strains would have been enormous. We were all 18 months to two years apart, with the last two being twin boys.

There is a part of me that understands completely why my father refused to let my mother, my sister and I go into Darling Harbour.

He did not consider it safe for females. On the rare occasion we did go, it would be on a Sunday when no one was around. I remember everything being dirty. The office was dirty; the platforms were dirty, the toilets were dirty and certainly completely unsuitable for women. I do remember seeing the "girlie" calendars on the walls around sheds.

Why then did I decide that I wanted to go to work with my father? My older brother could work for him, and it was intended that he learn the business with a view to succession planning. Working for the company was never an option for me. It was made perfectly clear by my grandfather and my uncle, and most certainly, Dad as well. My role was to be a wife and mother, and I would be "taken care of" by my husband. It was reinforced when the boys in the family all had life insurance policies taken out … yes, the boys … not the girls!

What am I feeling? Anger. Anger that society could mistreat women so badly. Anger that I could be excluded from doing the one thing I wanted to do – which was to be successful in business. Anger that I was not allowed to do the things I wanted to do. Anger that I could be put down, discarded, like a second-hand piece of clothing. This develops into a rage I recognise I have felt for a long time. Rage which had to be suppressed because "I was a good girl" and "girls don't get angry." Rage, because I grew up believing that "men had all the knowledge"; that "men know best"; that "men will take care of me." Rage because inevitably not only did they know less than I did, they certainly didn't know best, and they most certainly didn't take care of me.

Even as I type these words, there is rage that society could perpetuate these lies, these rules. More so, that women and, by extension, me, have accepted them. We have been "sold a pup" (the translation of this idiom according to the Merriam Webster's Dictionary is *"to trick someone into paying too much for something or into buying something that is worthless"*) by Hollywood, and the movie industry.

All through society, there are situations where women receive less remuneration than men. In most jobs, men are paid more than women. In sporting events, men are paid more than women. In the movie industry, men are paid more than women.

There has been a widely held belief in society that women are not allowed to earn more than men. This belief is held by men, as well. Fortunately, it is slowly changing, and we experience situations men have chosen to become "stay at home dads" while their wives work.

It is only in recent times, and in very select circumstances where women are receiving equal pay. Ashleigh Barty, the Australian Women's tennis player, became the highest-paid women's tennis player in history when she won a tournament in Shenzhen, China, in November 2019. The Australian Women's Football team, the Matilda's, also secured a deal in November 2019 to share equally the commercial revenue from the Football Federation of Australia (FFA) with their male counterparts equally.

Recently I read an article about a young Jewish woman who had become a Rabbi. To quote from the ABC (Australia) "(Ellsye Borghi) ... recently received her ordination – or smicha in Hebrew – which qualifies her as the newest and second-ever Australian female Orthodox rabbi."[2] The article goes on to describe how unusual it is for a female to achieve such a prestigious position in the community. Ellyse has chosen to be known as a rabbanit, the Jewish name for a Rabbi's wife. I found the whole article incredible mainly because "Shuly Rubin Schwartz, a professor of Jewish history, describes the role of rabbanit – also known by its Yiddish title, rebbetzin – as derivative. You only get to have [the role] if you're married to a rabbi," she says, "and the prestige of the role, in many ways, parallels that of the rabbi." And "Dr Schwartz knows a thing or two about rabbis and their wives – her father was a rabbi, her son is a rabbi, and she was married to a rabbi for 24 years." The piece I found fascinating was when Dr Schwartz said: "For most of the 20th century, the idea of marriage and career were seen as incompatible ... the closest way you could get to what you wanted was to marry what you wanted to be."

So it is with most religions and religious institutions. Breaking through the rules, beliefs and boundaries which have governed us as women is still an almost impossible task. There are still societies where women are suppressed.

There are still women who believe that they need to be taken care of. This is a rage I have not been able to shift in all the work I have done. I had such a drive to be successful, and this belief

---

2. https://www.abc.net.au/news/2019-09-22/ellyse-borghi-isnt-a-rabbi-or-a-rabba-shes-a-rabban-it/11520114

that I'm not allowed to be successful has caused me so much pain and anguish. It was reinforced by my mother, who believed that for me to be accepted in society I should learn to contain my ambitions and focus them on being the best hostess. I should learn the social skills which could benefit my husband to be successful. I should learn to cook and entertain, and encourage my husband to entertain his business contacts at home. I'm surprised that she didn't send me to "finishing school," although she did send me to elocution and deportment classes where I learned to speak and walk "the correct way." This possibly came from her own struggle to fit into a small-town society where she was never really able to break the social stigma of being "blue collar."

The power of beliefs

Is it possible that a fear of success also underlies some of what I have described? Is it possible that Mum was afraid that if I became more successful than my husband, it would create conflict? The more I open into this possibility, the more I can hear Mum's fear. She came from an era when women were subservient to their husbands and certainly could not stand on their own. She only had a voice in the home – with her own children – it was a voice that could only be heard in that environment, nowhere else, which led to the beliefs she espoused. She would have been surprised to find a man targeting a woman because of her wealth.

Beliefs are such strong drivers, even when society changes,

beliefs still seem to be deeply embedded in our DNA. Beliefs need not necessarily be spoken. They can be unwritten, accepted as normal, handed down from generation to generation. It can be traditions that imbed the belief, it can be "just accepted" by cultures; or simply "because it was good enough for my mother, it's good enough for me."

Words matter. Beliefs matter. They impact us on a very deep level because, generally, they are false and self-limiting. When we take on beliefs – whether they be from our family of origin, our adopted families, our partners, our religion, our corporate organisations, or our politics – they all impact us.

Every person with whom I have worked over the past 20 years has uncovered unhealthy beliefs. Beliefs that have held them back from achieving the things they most want to do in life.

In one coaching session, a client made the following statement:

> Every negative thought creates a story which creates pain. Pain reinforces hate and loathing, which I keep having to create even more stories, which reinforces the negativity, which reinforces the story, which keeps me small and unhappy. All of this keeps me behind the wall I have created to protect myself, which keeps me sheltered, which reinforces the separation I feel from others, which reinforces the belief that I don't deserve connection.

Can you read the turmoil which is created? We all have beliefs that are doing this to us all the time.

♡

EXERCISE

In this case, the client described the wall he had built around himself. His wall was 6 foot (182 cm) tall, 5 metres (16.5 feet); yes, he did confuse the measurements between metric and imperial. I asked if there were any sides to the wall, how far did they extend? He explained they extended forever, and I also asked what's behind the wall? And he said there was a void.

During the session, I continued to ask what was the wall preventing him from receiving? His answer was Love – Life; what was the wall preventing him from giving? Again, his answer was Love, Joy, Appreciation. The next question I asked was, "What is the wall preventing you from being?" He answered, "Me; seeing me, wearing the clothes I want to wear; being successful."

When asked whether the wall was doing the job it was initially erected for, he said, "No, it is doing the exact opposite." When asked what needed to happen to the wall, he said, "It needs to be removed."

We then went through a process of knocking the wall down with a figurative "ball and chain," clearing away the debris and coming to a beautiful place of forgiveness of self where he was able to feel the breeze around him, to feel the fresh air.

In my case, I discovered that I had an igloo around me. It was made of very strong blocks of ice. It had a small entrance which I could crawl through, or let someone in if I wanted to – and this rarely happened. I knew I had an icy exterior. My interactions with people were always cold. I felt very little love. I had felt hurt in my relationship, and I was never going to let anyone in again. I had made a strong vow that I would never be hurt again, and this wall was my protection. This vow had caused me to put on weight to make myself undesirable to men. When I became aware of the vow, I went through a simple process of releasing myself from it; then, I needed to get a figurative "blow torch" and melt the igloo from the inside out. The changes that occurred as a result of this simple process were that I felt my heart open, and I could be compassionate and loving of others as well as myself.

What happens in the mind when we take these actions is that the neural pathways are reset. Bruce Lipton describes in Chapter 6 of *The Biology of Belief* that we have some survival techniques which help us grow and which provide us with safety. He goes on to describe that there are times when we go into protection mode, and alternatively, we also need to grow and that these techniques are unable to operate at the same time.

Letting go of old rules, beliefs and vows that no longer support us stimulates the growth process, which leads us to be open to more choices and, therefore, more fulfilling lives.

To believe that, as a woman, I had only one role in life, and to discover, after 18 months, that the man I married was infertile, was very confronting – what was my role now? Although I was subsequently fortunate to adopt two adorable boys and to raise them to be wonderful citizens of the world, there was, for a very long time, a yearning within that could not be fulfilled. What I didn't understand was the impossible bind I was living with – on the one hand, I believed my only role was to be a mother, and on the other, I longed to be a successful businesswoman. The conflict between these two, led to an even deeper belief, that as a woman I have no value. If I have no value, is it possible for me to be successful? The obvious answer is no, and if success were on the horizon, something would always occur to sabotage it.

Holding onto the belief that as a woman I was not allowed to be successful has held me back for most of my life. Twice I have had successful businesses, and on both occasions, I have lost them. In the first case, I can choose to blame the 1991 recession that Paul Keating (Prime Minister 1991–1996) said "we had to have"; and the second one I can choose to blame an ex-husband who almost bankrupted me. Or I can accept the responsibility that my beliefs played a major role. I'm sure that the quote at the head of this chapter is where the real issue lies. This message became a belief by which I have lived. I truly believed that I could be the "power behind the throne." I truly believed that I could help my husband be successful, and then he would take care of me, and I would feel I had succeeded in my life's purpose. I cringe when I write those words as they are now so alien to me. I cringe because I see the impact those words had on my life. They caused me to live in two toxic relationships, which completely undermined my very existence. Even when I had a period of 18 years as a single person, I still felt incomplete. Without a husband, I had no value, and I could not be successful.

Maybe I am a slow learner – It took me a long time to become aware that I needed to change my beliefs. The first opportunity for me to look at beliefs came when I discovered The Journey, a healing modality pioneered by Brandon Bays. Brandon understood the power beliefs have in our lives. As part of the practitioner certification, two of the four programs proved enlightening – one called Conscious Abundance and the other Healing with Conscious Communication. During both of these seminars, I undertook several belief change processes. The power of these processes was palpable. I got to recognise that I could let go of beliefs that I have held onto; and which I could now forget.

I could create the life I wanted.

When we change our beliefs, when we let them go, everything around us changes. We let go of being a victim. We are victims when we hold fast to the beliefs such as "I'm not good enough"; "there's no way out of it,"; "I'm a waste of space"; "I can't get on with my life"; "I'm not a good friend"; "I'm too serious"; "I'm not social enough"; "I'm not good enough technically"; "I'm not intellectual"; I'm too constrained" – the list is endless. There is so much freedom to be experienced without the baggage of beliefs.

So, what does success look like? For that matter, what does failure look like? We all judge success, and more importantly, we all judge failure, particularly our own. I can look at two marriages that lasted nine years and 14 years respectively. Do I count them as failures? At one time, yes, I did. Do I now? No. I count them as huge learning curves, which taught me a lot about human nature. I count them as blessings, as from each I have gained so much. From the first, I gained two beautiful sons, as well as three adorable granddaughters. From the second, I gained two awesome grandsons – I could call them step-grandsons, and I choose to ignore the "step" part. I also gained a couple of daughters-in-law with whom I have fantastic relationships. Is that a failure – absolutely not.

Success or failure

Again, what does success look like? For more than ten years, I have had my own company, and I feel very satisfied with the success achieved. Does it mean financial success? You can have all the financial wealth in the world and be unhappy. I can joke and say that some more financial success would be good, and I can honestly say, I'm working on it! Being happy is a much better measure of success. Health is a much better measure of success. Friendship is a much better measure of success. Being at peace with myself is an even better measure of success.

Did I fail to achieve in some of the many endeavours I have attempted along the way? Some of them possibly, and in each, there has been a gift. It has certainly been challenging going through the process, particularly the process of letting go of my two marriages, there were very expensive financial lessons, and I know that I have grown as a result.

In mid-2017, I set out on a solo trip to Spain with the intention of walking the Camino de Santiago. I intended to walk the majority of the 770 kilometres – albeit I was starting in Pamplona instead of St Jean Pied de Port at the base of the Pyrenees. Being aware of the limitations of my body, my age, and my physical health, I felt that it was judicious that I take it relatively easy. As with all pilgrimages, most of the challenges are spontaneous, and so it was for me. I was three days into my walk, having stayed the night in an Albergue (hostel) in Puente la Reina, a beautiful small village in the Navarre region, I set out along the trail to walk to the next village to where my small bag had been despatched. All of a sudden, I found myself stumbling and unable to control anything. I fell to the ground.

I was OK. I just knew I could not continue walking, and what do I do? I was alone. Well, that was true for about a minute. Then two lovely young women from Alaska came along and made sure I was OK. Then four other people from different nationalities, including an Australian, came upon us; they also rendered assistance and discussed how they could get me to the main road so I could get some help. Out of nowhere, we all turned around, and there was a red police car! It literally appeared. No sound, no nothing, on the narrow stretch of track. They put me in the back – on very uncomfortable moulded plastic seats (for obvious reasons!); they generously opened the windows (there were no door or window handles) and drove me back to Puente la Reina to a medical centre where they stayed with me to ensure I was in good hands. The doctor examined me and determined that my blood pressure was high and made the suggestion that I find an alternative to walking on my own.

As I was determined to continue my pilgrimage, I decided to do it by modern-day horse (a bus!). It is common for people to cycle the Camino. There was no attachment to achieving the pilgrim's passport full of stamps acquired along the way and the ultimate certificate of completion at the Cathedral in Santiago de Compostela. It was more important that I enjoyed and survived the journey.

When I reflect on my initial decision to go to Spain, I had researched the possibility of getting to Lourdes (in southern France); to Fatima in Portugal, and to a small village called Avila about 100 kilometres outside of Madrid. All of these did not initially fit into my itinerary, and all of these were able to be manifested because of my fall.

It is possible for me to look at my not walking the Camino as a failure. I choose to see it differently. As a result of my "accident" my pilgrimage became even more meaningful by being able to experience the magnificent countryside of northern Spain; being able to spend time in exploring the history of the Camino and the churches and Cathedrals along the Way. More importantly, I had the chance to visit Lourdes at a very auspicious time (a major feast day in the Catholic calendar) and to get to Fatima – a place I have longed to see for most of my life. I also got to visit Avila, which has special meaning to one of my aunts, who was a Carmelite nun for most of her life (it is the birthplace of St Theresa who founded the Order). Without "my incident," these are places that would still be on my bucket list.

We underestimate the power of intent – the power of what you focus on; to manifest. If you focus on the negative, that is what you will manifest. If you focus on the positive, then that is what you will get.

Sharing a home with my daughter-in-law and granddaughters presents some interesting occasions to meet the various aspects of how life plays out. For one of the girls' birthday, I decided I

would love to make a cheesecake recipe I had seen on Pinterest. The ingredients called for some Maltesers (for decoration) and Malteser Spread, which is only available in the United Kingdom. A quick YouTube search came up with an alternative. The birthday duly arrived, and I set about making this delicacy. As cheesecake is a family favourite, I was sure I was on a winner. Everything came together … until the construction time arrived. I took the cheesecake out of the springform tin and mounted it on a cake stand, then proceeded to layer the spread over it. From that point on, my beautiful creation became a monumental disaster. The spread dripped down the cheesecake and onto the kitchen bench. The Maltesers, which were supposed to be the "pièce de résistance" on the top, joined the spread on the kitchen bench. I surrendered. There was nothing to be done to rescue the creation. My granddaughter arrived home and came over with a spoon and hoed into it, stating how amazing it was, and she was going to enjoy it irrespective of the look. I took the opportunity of sharing with both my daughter-in-law and granddaughter that in the past, I would have been stressed and panicky because it "wasn't right," the cake "didn't look good enough." The truth is, it really didn't matter what it looked like. It tasted delicious, and while I would have preferred it to have been otherwise, we all enjoyed laughing at the result and connecting as we licked the caramelly mess from the bench.

Was it a failure? I could have thrown it out and gone to the local patisserie for something equally delicious, and we would have missed out deeply connecting over caramel on the kitchen bench. I know which one I prefer.

At the end of each financial year, some companies do a stocktake – which lists the inventory the business holds. Have you ever considered doing a stocktake of your life? List the tangible and intangible things you have – such as the love and acceptance of family and friends; the good relations you have with work colleagues; the amazing skills you have gained; the things you have learned. The gifts in the failures you have experienced. Be grateful for all these and experience what changes when you are in gratitude.

To be successful and to grow, we have to step outside our comfort zones. I have been fortunate to have seen the numerous changes which have taken place with office technology. When I first began my working life, I learned to type on a typewriter.

When I established a secretarial business, in 1981, I purchased a "state of the art" golf ball typewriter. To change the font, you had to insert a new "golf ball" typeface.

Very soon after, new "state of the art" equipment was introduced, and I had to move to a Xerox Memory Writer, which stored the information on floppy disks. The program for the machine was on a floppy inserted into the left-hand slot at the base of the keyboard, and the information was stored on a floppy on the right-hand side.

There were so many machines I purchased over the ten year life of my business (and subsequently) as technology changed the entire workplace in which I operated. My point is that to succeed, I had to adapt to change as it occurred. I could have stayed with the original cumbersome typewriter, or I could move with the times and adapt and learn. My beliefs could have kept me from exploring the way technology could help me … such as now, learning to use the various apps on my smartphone and iPad, which make my life enjoyable, or I could throw my arms in the air and limit the things I can do.

♡

EXERCISE

Recently a new form of technology triggered my "fear of being incompetent" button. (This one came out of nowhere). I have been using accounting software for a very long time. I have had to adapt to new programs along the way, and felt confident that having mastered many things in my life this would be another one I could manage. I had completely underestimated the way the program worked and felt completely out of my depth. When I feel this way, the first thing I resort to is food. On this particular day, even food reacted in my body. I hate this feeling of being incompetent. It brings tears to my eyes and is so debilitating. I want to distract myself entirely. I want to stop writing and find something else to do. The more I "sit" with this emotion, the more I can feel it in my stomach. It feels like a churning – a bit like a front loader washing machine tossing and turning everything around. I have nowhere to go. The fear originates from having to repeat Year 4 at high school (we had five years in high school). My grades for English were considered insufficient to get through the final year, and the teachers recommended to my parents that I repeat. This is that feeling – I have been judged to be incompetent.

I want to vomit, and yet I want to drink something, so this feeling goes away, and I know if I do, I will lose the opportunity to deal with this finally. I wipe away the tears and blow my nose; let's deal with this now. The 17-year-old me believed that she was incompetent because she could not understand what the hell Shakespeare was saying when he wrote King Lear (and Twelfth Night). I also could never understand the language of poets. My thinking was "why can't they say it in plain English" (and I am aware of the word "can't" in this context!). Scrapping through my final year at school, I went onto Secretarial College, where I studied shorthand and typing and, ultimately, accounting.

One of the roles in my working life was as Executive Assistant to three senior executives of a very large multinational business. Years later, I finally accepted that, in this role, I achieved a "degree in reading lousy handwriting"!! and, more importantly, that I corrected, not only the spelling and also the English and comprehension of these three male executives – I made them look good!!! Maybe this is what Mum actually meant when she said I could be "the power behind the throne."

We don't know what we don't know

One of the beautiful reflections I have had on the Keys to Success Over Failure is there are times when I don't know what I don't know. And I can't know what I don't know until I know what I need to know.

Can I explain it this way? When I started recently with the new software, I believed there were two programs involved and did the research on both to understand how they operated. When that research appeared to be inadequate, I had to ask for help and get some training. At the training, I "discovered" there was something wrong, as the information in the accounting program was not up to date. It wasn't synced with the database correctly. It was then I found that there was a syncing program that bought them both together. The error was in this syncing program. I could "blame" or sit in judgment on myself for not knowing, or accept that I didn't know what I didn't know. With this realisation, there is no blame for incompetence as there is no incompetence. I just didn't know what I didn't know.

How much nicer would it be if society set us up for SUCCESS as opposed to the opposite?

Now, Mum, it's time for me to sit on my own throne. It's time for me to step into my own power and to accept and acknowledge that I am allowed to be successful in my own right. I can achieve anything to which I put my attention. I am still hungry for that success. I have the strength and capability to wear the crown of success. It is time to listen to my own words of success and pay attention to them.

CHAPTER 3

How What You Say Manifests
Health or Disease

♡

*Every human being is the author of his
own health or disease.*

Buddha

CHAPTER 3

How What You Say Manifests Health or Disease

No matter how much it gets abused, the body can restore balance.

The first rule is to stop interfering with nature.

Deepak Chopra

The first quote contains tough words that I have increasingly questioned as I progress through my life. The second is one I believe and one to which I can attest.

The one thing I can be sure of is that I cannot know what causes one person to have good health and another to have disease. I can never know why one child can be healthy and another sick.

It's my choice

What I do have an understanding of is that if I choose to drink alcohol and end up damaging my liver, then that is my choice. If I choose to smoke cigarettes or take other substances, and my

lungs get damaged, then that is my choice. Equally, I know that if I choose to live with toxic anger and resentment, then that too has an effect on my body, and that also is my choice. If I choose to live with fear, and in a constant state of being "on guard," consistently drawing down on my adrenals, then that too is going to deplete my body, and that is also my choice. I have also come to realise that when I shut down or shut out emotions, that too is my choice and will have some effect on my body as well.

The common denominator here is CHOICE! As an adult, I make a choice – whether that be a conscious choice or an unconscious choice – I am still choosing. Choices occur through internal statements, thoughts, beliefs, vows, or determinations. I make a choice every time I say something. I can choose to speak in a judgemental, controlling, derogative or condescending manner. I can choose to speak in a kind and caring way. I can choose to speak warmly. I can choose to speak out of anger or fear. I can choose to speak out of hatred or out of love.

I choose how I interact with the world. I choose empathy or apathy. I can choose to integrate or withdraw. I choose to be involved, or I choose to be aloof.

One of the choices I made as a child and as a young adult was to shut down emotionally. It was a pattern I repeated many times in my life. Of course, I was not consciously aware of what I was doing at the time, I was trying to protect myself from a perceived threat, or from an emotion I didn't know how to handle. I also did not appreciate that all of these choices have consequences.

In chapter 2 on Success and Failure, I wrote about beliefs. One of the occasions I remember was when I grew up believing men had all the knowledge, that my life depended on a man, that what I wanted was totally and utterly dependent on what the males in my family and in the wider community, dictated; the belief I took on was that women had no value. I had what is called the "princess syndrome," I bought into the "fairy tale." I would marry my "knight in shining armour" and we would live happily ever after. This belief was reinforced when I was in my early teens when I received a letter (to this day, I am unable to recall the contents, as my mother took it straight away). It is my understanding that the letter contained details which led me to believe my grandfather, father and uncle (who were in business together), had taken out life insurance policies on all the boys in the two families (there were six children in my family, and seven in my uncles). The premise they used was that the girls would marry and "be taken care of" by their husbands. We didn't need life insurance.

It didn't help subsequently when Prince Charles married Princess Di, and the media went into a frenzy around them. The story being played out was that Princess Diana was "set for life" she had the dream every girl wanted. She had her prince, and she lived in a castle and even produced two beautiful sons. The monarchy had its heirs, and Diana was the toast of the entire world. She had to be happy.

Unfortunately, like most people, I didn't see the reality. I didn't see beyond the fairy tale. I bought into the media hype; I bought into the Hollywood dream; I bought into the make-believe. (It is strange that women still buy into the make-believe – probably one reason that rom-coms (romantic comedies) are the Number One genre in the movies). Some women believe they need to be taken care of, that their lives will be better, that they will be happy if they just had a man to take care of them.

After I left school, I attempted to do accountancy, which at that time was an evening college course. My challenge was that I was the only female in the class, and the men couldn't cope, and I was hounded out with comments – why would you bother studying – you will never need this qualification!

The body communicates

Why am I describing this? It was at this time I became aware that I felt shut down. I also felt myself shut down when I went on a date with a young man who was to become my husband. On this occasion we met in the city at a bar, he ordered a beer with a rum chaser. I had no idea what happened to me at that moment. I felt like I had been stabbed with a knife. It felt like a dagger going into the very pit of my stomach. I had no idea at the time why I reacted. It was such a strange reaction to someone ordering a drink, so I shut it down. I refused to listen to my body. Every time I experienced this sensation, I would repeat the shutdown cycle. I subsequently uncovered the reason for the collapse. My dad was an alcoholic, and, as a very young child, his favourite beverage was rum and milk. When he drank too much, he became angry and loud, and I felt afraid of him.

A few weeks later, we made arrangements for him to come to my home to visit and meet my parents. As he was an apprentice in the Royal Australian Navy and didn't have a car, he caught the train. I collected him from the station. At the end of the evening, the reverse happened. I drove him back to the station and just as we were saying goodbye I "threw up" – I vomited! (Thank God for the handkerchiefs I used to carry.) The same thing happened again a couple of weeks later. Yes, I felt very embarrassed and did my best to cover the evidence. My body was trying to tell me something; I shut down.

What I didn't know at the time, and describing it now it seems obvious, was that my body was experiencing a sensation. It is these sensations I have come to know as feelings. Feelings are a very important mechanism through which the body focusses our attention. Pain and discomfort are also important sensations the body has to warn us. Pain highlights that there is a problem. A good example is toothache – a warning that there is an issue in our mouths; or headache – a warning that maybe you need to have some water as you may be dehydrated – or some other reason. The best one for me is my leg aches when I have been walking around barefoot when I need to wear shoes as my arches have dropped, and I walk completely differently without the support of orthopaedics in my shoes.

CASE STUDY

Recently one of my dear friends, Suzanne, was describing how her son Andrew and his brother were having a rumble on the floor. Andrew got hurt and needed medical attention to get some stitches and dress the wound. His mum and dad disagreed where to take him. Mum wanted Andrew to go to the ER while Dad suggested he go to the local medical centre. Eventually, Dad ended up dropping Andrew alone at the local surgery, where he was able to get his wound dressed. While Andrew was at the doctor's, Dad went to the nearby supermarket to stock up on drinks, chips, and lollies – his way of avoiding the trauma of seeing his son with blood all over him; and not being able to deal with it emotionally. He shut down his emotions with a sugar fix. Most of us do the same; our "sugar fix" may be alcohol, drugs, or sex (yes, sex can also be an addiction).

Kaljit is an amazing man I have come to know over the past ten years or so. I first met him at a Journey Intensive, where he came seeking answers to an issue he had with alcohol. He has been "working" on this problem for most of that time, and occasionally he has some insights which give him the opportunity of putting down the booze for a few weeks, only to pick it up again when the next challenge arose. One day, he sent me a photo of a cousin's birthday party. Kaljit would have been about three years old at the time. The photo was of three women and six children. It could have been any photo of any child's birthday, except beside the birthday cake in this photo was a bottle of scotch whiskey. In his text, along with the photo, he wrote: *"Indian way of celebrating birthdays for the kids. Birthday cake, lots of sweets and a whiskey bottle with a dozen shot glasses* [for the female adults] *... we started too young. They used to rub whiskey in our mouths to put us to sleep."*

This comment may seem unremarkable on first reading. As a baby boomer, I recollect that it was common for parents to rub brandy on the gums of babies when they were teething, to numb the pain. The more I sat with this knowledge, the more I felt disturbed by it.

Our choices have consequences

Part of my role as a self-awareness coach is to "connect the dots." Everything in our lives has consequences. The words we speak have consequences; the behaviours we act out have consequences; our actions have consequences. Most of these consequences are inconsequential, others are more significant. The first time we speed in our cars and get caught, the consequence is an infringement notice and the potential loss of demerit points. The second time, something similar. When we get to the fourth or fifth speeding fine, then the consequences are greater. It is both expensive, and the potential for the immediate loss of licence or deprivation of liberty is even greater.

What I know from the work I have done with people is that our bodies store memories from a very young age, even in utero, and sometimes from past lives. (The common term for them is cellular memories.) What are the long-term consequences of the simple act of rubbing a child's inner cheek with whiskey or numbing a child's gum with brandy? Alcohol is a suppressant – which is the reason the mothers in Kaljit's photo rubbed it in their children's cheeks. It helped to quieten the children and put them to sleep. Brandy on the child's gums helped numb the pain of teething. It shut the children down. It is a form of shut down, this time from an external source.

Fast forward to being a teenager or young adult and emotions are going haywire – hormones are developing – and your first sip of whiskey or brandy (or your parent's favoured beverage) sends reminders to the subconscious of being calm, or numbing out, and the body craves more of it. Unfortunately, "more of it" has the opposite effect of calming – it stimulates and often brings about aggressive behaviour.

The Indian women (and men) who used alcohol with children, would more than likely be horrified that a simple act of trying to assist their child to get to sleep or to get some relief from pain, could have such disastrous consequences. And yet, it is the simple things we do and say that have these results.

Or is it more simple? Is it that none of us are taught how to deal with our emotions or pain, nor are we taught the impact of the words we say. None of us are taught very much about life and how to live it positively. There is no manual about how to live an amazing life. Mostly the words we hear more frequently are "No" and "Don't."

A dear friend John had a heart attack and was taken to the hospital. He has spent most of his life being totally opposed to conventional medicine and pills; as a matter of fact, he hates doctors and hospitals and resents the fact that he put himself in the position of needing their assistance. He believes he can heal himself without medical intervention. However, he needed a heart bypass to keep him alive. He also needed beta blockers to keep the blood flowing safely through his body. What the doctors and John didn't appreciate at the time is that he decided years ago that he hates pills, and he has told himself that he is "allergic" to them. So, what John does while he is in hospital is to say to himself, "I'm f****, I have no control over my life. I am completely controlled by others. It's a one-way trip, and it's all downhill from here." And he shuts down. Four months later, he discovers that he has fluid built up around his heart and legs, needs diuretics to remove the fluid, and he now needs to see a cardiologist. John has effectively shut down his entire life force – and the one thing he doesn't want to see is a doctor who is sure to tell him he needs even more medication. To complicate matters even more, subsequently, John develops severe pain and numbness in his knees and legs.

Death wishes

John and I have been having twice-weekly sessions and are constantly amazed at the hidden gems which arise as he opens into the consequences of his emotional shutdown as a young boy.

He is aware that we could be having a conversation, and he could say something, and I will hear a belief or a vow he had made in the past. One of those was a death wish. He had been forced to take phenobarbital and other drugs as a child. When he got to 14 years of age, he decided he had had enough and told his mother, "Stick your pills, I'm doing it my way." This simple act set up conflict within him. Some of the strong beliefs which arose at that time were: "No one can make me do anything I don't want to do"; "It's my way or the highway"; "If it's easy it isn't right"; and "I'll kill myself before I let you break me."

When the severe pain in his legs became challenging, we spent time concentrating on clearing whatever was stopping the flow. He went to have an ultrasound, where it was discovered that the artery supplying blood to the left leg was severely blocked. The sonographer was astounded that he hadn't lost his leg.

In the next session, we checked that the death wish he had made a long time ago had been cleared. What he uncovered was a "double bind." A double bind occurred when one part of him was saying, "It's not worth the ****ing trouble" and the other "You promised you would stay." These two statements are incongruent with each other and cause conflict in the body. He also subsequently uncovered some additional beliefs he took on after the surgery, including "I'll never walk again properly" and "It'll be hard to walk." He also uncovered that he was angry with the surgeon as he had not been informed before the operation about what was proposed. When he asked what needed to take place, the response came that he needed to surrender totally.

What does surrender mean? It means having no expectations around anything, surrendering to life. The words that came from John then were – "Pure Freedom, where everything is free to flow – free to be." Then he said, with a smile, "I can live with this."

Remembering John's death wish, I asked him to repeat, "I can LIVE with this." The more he spoke the words, the more he realised the importance of them. "I can LIVE with this … This freedom."

Next, I asked him to allow this freedom to wash through every artery, vein and capillary in his body, particularly focussing on the lower limbs. He had his eyes closed all this time, and opened into … in his words "huge openness, huge freedom." He went on to forgive himself for doubting.

Death wishes are very common. Kaljit also had one. He felt he was a disappointment to his family. He had to deal with a lot of cultural issues, particularly around an arranged marriage. He had a belief he would be disowned if he didn't want to get married; he was afraid of his father's anger. He also had a fear of getting angry; and getting things wrong, fear of getting into trouble when he was a child – as his father would hit him. He lived with this fear most of his life. It left him hating people. He described it this way "I could be speaking to someone and the next minute (in my mind) I could be slapping people, and the next moment I would go silent and shut down. I felt like I don't belong here; my life is shit. I have pushed this down – it makes me feel sad; it makes me feel there is something wrong with me." He also witnessed his uncle coming between two cousins, urging one to hit the other and saying it wasn't hard enough. Kaljit said, "The look in my uncle's eyes was terrifying."

In a call with Kaljit, he says that death is at his doorstep. "I'm running from life. I have not realised that even this is a death wish. I said, 'I'm fucked'; I use words like this every day. 'I wish I were dead'; 'Life is too hard'. I was not aware of the number of times I say this every day. I'm cancelling out all the work I've done by these death wishes. I took on my parent's beliefs. I haven't lived my life to the fullest, because I didn't want to disappoint my parents. You leave this house you are cut off from life. Every time I was in a relationship, I couldn't be IN the relationship until I had my parent's approval." Kaljit's cousin, Raj, also had an issue with alcohol. He lost everything – his business, his wife, and his children. He spent time on the streets homeless as he ostracised everyone. He would say, "I'm out of here" over and over – Kaljit now realises how powerful death wishes are. Raj eventually succumbed to his alcoholism and passed away.

Remember Suzanne? It was only in hindsight she was able to see what played out that night with Andrew. She has become more aware of the way the family is interacting and has since had discussions with her husband, and the boys. They can now deal with their emotions positively and openly.

We have to be very careful about the words we speak. When we make comments such as "This is killing me"; or "I'd die for a pizza"; or even "I'd rather be dead" or even "F*** this life," we have no awareness of the consequences.

A well-known Australian saying is "bugger me dead" (an ex-husband used to say this until I stopped him by telling I had no intention of him dying while we were having intercourse!). There are so many more of them. Please be careful with anything you say. The Universe will hear you and will grant your wish. You may not mean it exactly as you are saying it, and I can guarantee you, the power you have to manifest is unable to differentiate between what you say and what you mean.

Can you undo a death wish? Yes, you can, please do it sooner rather than later. The longer you leave a death wish in place, the more difficult it is to change, and the body is capable of manifesting anything.

Find a Journey Practitioner and ask them to do a Vow and Belief Change process with you – or you can find some tools to help on my website ... www.janhenderson.com.au.

John's way of finally clearing his death wish was to repeat a mantra for the next seven days, "I can LIVE with this Freedom." We know that it takes time to change a habit, and this is the same, we need to embed the new belief/vow, and saying it over and over in the form of a mantra is one way.

Holding onto secrets

We all have secrets? What is the emotional and physical impact of these secrets on our bodies?

Are there topics that can never be spoken about in your family? The one subject around which there is most taboo is sex and our sexuality. Whether it is through embarrassment, shame, or lack of knowledge on the part of our parents, it is something about which no one wants to talk. It is a "no-go" zone.

If you or your parents have a religious background, it is possibly even more taboo. Churchgoers will have been pontificated to from the pulpit about the condemnation of God's wrath brought on with the advent of sexual development. The "dangers" of masturbation for both males and females. For boys, it is particularly confusing with the changes taking place in their bodies as their voices "break," testicles drop, and penis enlarges are confusing. If the sensations experienced are unable to be explained, then where do kids turn?

I have lost count of the number of men I have counselled who have said to me that their first sexual experience was a "non-event" brought about through anxiety, apprehension, and sheer terror of what might or might not happen. The embarrassment causes performance anxiety throughout their lives – an occasion which is supposed to be joyous turns out to be a complete disaster.

For women, too, there is much anxiety. In my case, Mum could not even discuss menstruation with me (and presumably my sister). When I first got my period, I thought I was bleeding to death. It was when she discovered me going to the medicine cabinet for cotton wool that she asked me what I needed it for, that she explained this would happen to me each month for most of my life, and she provided me with the necessary pads. End of discussion. That was it. Nothing more. No discussion about other parts of my body which would have strange reactions. Let alone what happens to boys as they develop. I have no memory of when I "discovered" that aspect of puberty. I do remember being horrified the first time I saw a fully erect penis. I wanted to run a mile. Then my husband to be wanted me to do other things with it. I felt mortified. Is there any way anyone can prepare for this experience? I know that I still have the memory.

During a television program, a woman (whom I will call Ann – not her real name) wanted to contact her birth mother. She had felt very supported by her adopted mother and father, and yet there was a yearning to meet the woman who gave birth to her. To do so, she hired a private investigator. This investigator made a discreet approach to a person who fitted the description and timeline, and he was told: "I have never told anyone about the birth, and I have a family now and not willing to go there." As the story goes, Ann wrote the birth mother a letter pleading her case for contact. Probably because it was a television show, this one had a happy ending – the birth mother relented and presumably (because it wasn't disclosed on the show) she had to fess up to her family about events more than 40 years ago. While I'm not suggesting in this case that there is any medical impact on this woman, it does raise the question for me about the emotional and physical influences of holding onto a secret? There are thousands of women who have secret abortions, secret pregnancies. Some of these have the opportunity of being discovered through the advances of DNA – what are the consequences of the stress this has on women. What about secret affairs? About sexual abuse;

physical abuse; emotional abuse; people who steal from their employers; who hold secrets from loved ones; what about the subjects that are taboo in families? All of this holding has to be stored somewhere. It doesn't go away.

What does this stress cause in our bodies? I know from personal experience that I was holding onto a secret, and the consequences caused me to have elevated blood pressure, which ultimately resulted in a mini-stroke (a TIA, a transient ischaemic attack). Fortunately for me, the TIA came in the form of slurred speech, and I was able to get immediate medical help, as it could have resulted in a full-blown stroke. Even after the TIA, I still held onto the secret and continued to have high blood pressure. It only released when I was able to write about the events I was holding onto, and the "secret" was no secret anymore.

This "holding" needs to be released. It needs to be "spoken" in some way. It needs to be told – and this can happen in a variety of ways.

In my role as a coach, I have been privileged to be on the receiving end of many secrets that have never previously been shared. The relief people feel when they unburden themselves is palpable. Their entire body relaxes, and lines are released from their faces. The "edge" they previously had is gone, and these are only the outward signs of the revealing, I cannot know the internal workings of the body. I can only guess the changes that can take place.

♡

EXERCISE

Using a journal is a great way of releasing the secret. It is a miraculous way of confessing our "sins." There is freedom in confessing; it does work. It appears from the television show that Ann's birth mother was able to share her secret with her present family, as her three daughters were on the show, and able to embrace the older sister with warmth and affection.

The body has the power to heal

One of the amazing things about The Journey and Journeywork is the opportunity to be released from trauma – both childhood and adult trauma. The freedom experienced when it is let go is palpable. There is a joy, there is peace. When the trauma is released, the body can relax, and the internal mechanism, which is so powerful, can operate in the manner it was designed. The body can repair itself.

A couple of years ago, I had a rotator-cuff injury to my shoulder (a rotator cuff injury is usually a strain or tear of the rotator cuff – the muscles, tendons, and joint capsule that stabilises your

shoulder. Injury often involves a tear to the rotator cuff tendons which are the thick bands of tissue that connect the muscles to the bones). A visit to the doctor and an ultrasound was in order, and the diagnosis was that the only remedy was surgery. I specifically asked the doctor whether the body could heal the injury by itself. The response was No – surgery was the only option. Using The Journey tools, I processed the anger around having to shoulder the financial responsibility for my life, rather than having to share that responsibility with a partner. As I am writing this book, I am here to tell you that the body can heal itself. I have full use of my arm, and the tendons have repaired. There is just freedom, and I can latch up my bra behind my back with both arms – no surgery! What I also did was to take some turmeric capsules to ease the inflammation and some magnesium to relax the muscles.

Your body is a power mechanism. It can heal – is it possible that conventional medicine is necessary? Absolutely. One of my clients had a tumour on his liver. We did some Journeywork, and at one point, he was admitted to ICU to have a stent put into the tumour so that the dead cancer cells could leach out. The family had been called to say their goodbyes. The last I heard from him was that he was back at work and enjoying life.

Is it possible to promise healing? No! That is one thing I cannot do. I can make no promises about anything. I am responsible for my life, and you are responsible for yours. I cannot know your destiny, just as you cannot know mine or anyone else's. All I can do is to make you aware of your thoughts and what you are saying. The rest is up to you.

CHAPTER 4

The Secrets to Self-Esteem Over Self Harm

♡

Take care how you speak to yourself
— because you are listening

Centre for Pastoral Care, Virginia

CHAPTER 4

The Secrets to Self-Esteem Over Self Harm

There is a direct correlation between the words we speak and the thoughts we have about ourselves and our self-esteem. There is also a direct correlation between self-esteem and how we value ourselves.

Our self-talk causes us so much pain and anguish. We tell ourselves we are unlikeable when we feel rejected at school; we tell ourselves there must be something wrong with me when the "cool group" rejects our efforts to belong; we despise ourselves when we make choices that may affect others (even though we know it is supportive for us); we blame ourselves for perceived hurt to others; we dress according to the latest fashion when another style would be more suitable; we constantly try hard to do the "right thing" only for it to be never enough for a parent to love us; we do things to make others happy, so they, in turn, will like/love us.

So often, we tell ourselves we are dumb when our teachers tried to instil concepts into our young heads, which we cannot grasp. We pretend to be strong when we feel vulnerable; we pretend to be happy when we are sad; we pretend to like someone or something when we dislike it. All this does is create internal conflict. We may not recognise it, and yet it is there.

www.JanHenderson.com.au

It is this conflict that underpins the way we act and react in the world. It lies at the very heart of our interactions with people every moment of every day.

Trust and betrayal

Two weeks before my mum passed away in October 1994, she said to me, "Can you ever forgive me for what happened at your First Communion?" It was 47 years earlier, and I was seven years old, my Mum was pregnant with my twin brothers, she had toxaemia (blood poisoning) and had been confined to bed for the most of the pregnancy. My communion was exactly a month before my brothers were born. Mum got out of bed, dressed my siblings and me, and we all went to Church. At that time, there was a communion breakfast at the convent after the Mass, and after the obligatory photos, we all proceeded over the road. Being on her feet for all that time would have been a strain on Mum, and so she asked Dad to take her home – leaving me all alone with the other children and their parents, to finish the "party." Dad was supposed to come back for me. Instead, he had made arrangements to go and look at a house he and Mum were buying for us as we needed more room. He got a little carried away with time and completely forgot about me. The party finished, and as Dad had not appeared, I decided to walk home. I cried most of the way, as I had to walk through a very scary park full of ghost gums. The one thing I do remember is getting to the corner of the street and seeing the car pulling out of the driveway. I have no memory of my thoughts on the way home; I know that I would have felt afraid.

This incident has impacted my life in so many ways. It set up a pattern for me – yes, the conflict within – where I would do anything for anyone rather than feeling abandoned. It also set up that I trust no one. If I can't trust my Dad, who can I trust? If I trust "you," you will not only abandon me; you will also betray me.

More importantly, I felt so angry with Dad, that I "made him pay!!!" I stole some coins out of the very large coin jar he kept in his cupboard. In turn, this has set up one way I express my anger – instead of voicing it by yelling and screaming, I will manipulate a situation, I exact revenge quietly and subtly – and the target person may never know it was me (I justified my actions by saying to myself that he had so many coins in the jar he would not have missed a few!). There is an even further connection to this; I used the coins I stole to buy lollies at the tuckshop – thus reinforcing the need for sugar when I am angry. I reach for anything that contains carbohydrates and sugar; I may not even realise that I am angry until I am feeling so uncomfortable with a sugar overdose that I begin to question what have I just done – such a revelation. The deeper realisation is that I took on not trusting myself. I learned never to trust myself. I had the outward persona of being a "good girl," but inside I was naughty – I was evil, I was a thief, so how could anyone trust me, how could I trust myself? These are the very words that impacted my self-esteem for so long and created such an internal conflict.

Trusting someone has such deep consideration in all aspects of our lives. Can you trust when you tell someone something

in confidence they will hold that information? Can you trust that someone will honour you by keeping the information to themselves? How do you feel when a bank or institution sells your private information? How do you feel when you tell Mum or Dad something personal, and they go and share with other family members? How do you feel when your brother or sister shares private information? How do you feel when someone close reads your private journal? How do you feel when your boss appears to withhold support? How do you feel when you have supported someone, and they turn their back on you?

There is an even deeper question, which is why do we break the trust people place in us? And more importantly, how do we feel when we break someone's trust? What do we get out of divulging the information we have about someone?

The way it appears to me, at least initially, is it gives us an ego boost. It boosts us when we have information no one else appears to have. It gives us currency. It makes us feel important. There is a temporary rush of adrenaline when we tell people information they may not already know.

If we feel undervalued, we feel small and insignificant. One way of boosting ourselves is to "sell information." It is a transaction – I'll tell you what I know in exchange for you (the receiver) giving me a response (such as "Oh, I didn't know that"), which in turn boosts my sense of me (I know something they don't know). When we deconstruct the cost of this "sale," the word that comes to me is BETRAYAL! We are betraying a trust someone has placed in us. How does this make us feel? The word "WORTHLESS" arises.

Ultimately this puts us in a loop – the more we betray someone – the more we need validation – the more we divulge, the more we need to be boosted, and so the loop continues. What we are manifesting, each time we speak about others and gossip or provide information given to us in confidence, is worthlessness. If we are creating worthlessness, it becomes impossible to feel valued. The simplest antidote to this is to stop gossiping. This simple act will change how you feel about yourself and others. You may have to expand the subjects you discuss, or you could learn to be okay with silence. In this way, you become more aware of your own self and your own worth.

Let's explore our sense of worth in a more basic way. Say, for example, you want to get a job or set up your own business, how do you put a value on your services if you feel worthless? You will always be asking am I charging too much, or am I charging too little? How much is someone going to pay me for what I am doing?

CASE STUDY

Tanya is a beautiful young woman who is doing the same writing program as me. We are both from Melbourne and have bonded over the writing exercise over the past few months. She called one morning to talk to me about some issues she was having about valuing her services. She went on to describe an experience she had the day before when a woman she had been working with deleted her as a Facebook friend. During the conversation, Tanya slipped the words "I didn't want to spend any more time with this girl" into the conversation, almost as an after-thought. These "little sound bites" ring loudly in my ears, when spoken by clients, grabbing my attention (note I wanted to say the negative … "can't be ignored"!) When I brought them to Tanya's awareness, I asked her, "What have you manifested?" She took some time to think through the question. It was then the realisation came. She had manifested exactly what she had wanted. She didn't have to speak them out, she just had to think them, and the Universe heard her, and it happened.

We then went onto explore what was really going on. We explored the conversation Tanya had had with her client/ friend. It appears that Tanya had spent a lot of time doing some kinesiology with this woman and had explained all the oils the woman needed to balance the things going on in her life. Several appointments had been booked and cancelled, and Tanya has spent a lot of time speaking with her friend, with no money or exchange happening. Then during the last conversation, Tanya had suggested purchasing a book online, and she even mentioned that she was writing a book and had one already available as an eBook for free. It was at this point that the client/ friend took the action of deleting or blocking her on Facebook– there had been no opportunity for a rational conversation.

♡

EXERCISE

Working with Tanya, I asked her, "What's the worst that would happen if she arrived at the school, and this woman turned her back on her and had wanted nothing to do with her?" Tanya responded that she would feel rejected and not liked. Again, I asked her, "How would it feel if you were never liked again, what's the worst that would happen?" After a couple of times of asking this question, she got to, "I'd feel dumb and stupid." This "little gem" came from teachers who told her when she was a child, she was dumb and stupid. She had felt triggered because here she is writing a book, expecting it to be the opportunity which will benefit her in a whole variety of ways, and underlying is a belief that she is dumb and stupid, so how would anyone value what she has written and purchase her book.

"Valuing me" set us both on a further exploration of how do we value "me?" I explained it to Tanya this way: she felt comfortable calling me and asking for my help because, in return, she is going to do some graphic design work for me with my marketing brochures. In this way, there is an exchange of time and value. She is acknowledging that she can ask me for help, and I feel comfortable in offering help because I know that she is doing something for me. It felt comfortable in the body. There is an even exchange. Much like having a cup of coffee – I ask for the coffee and pay over my $5 for it, and the café proprietor provides me with it. There is an exchange taking place, and it feels comfortable in the body.

In the case of Tanya's friend – the exchange was one way, leaving Tanya feeling drained of energy – and the friend simply taking and offering nothing in return. It is a physical reaction – Tanya describes it as heavy. For me, it is depleting I feel exhausted when this happens.

We also explored another layer of this complex situation where value comes in. Tanya also had a judgment about her friend's ability to pay. She assumed that her friend didn't have the money to pay. This assumption is a common judgment. We feel sorry for people who want something and appear not to have the financial resources available. We give and give because we feel sorry for the other person. Sometimes we do it out of compassion, and yet there needs to be an exchange of energy. I learned this lesson a very long time ago when I worked in the accounts office for a lighting manufacturer. Often people would walk into the showroom, and if the sales staff were unavailable, I would have to step in and attempt to advise on lights for what could be for a single room or a whole house or even a whole building. One day a man walked in and, to use one of my grandfather's favourite phrases, "He looked like he didn't have two bob to rub together." I was very pleasant and offered the assistance I could. Later the marketing manager related that this particular man was

extremely wealthy and was building a "serious mansion," and the value to the business was enormous. I felt astounded. To mix my metaphors that day, I learned ... "never judge a book by its cover." I can never really know the financial resources to which others have access.

Valuing oneself, and others even comes down to asking for help. It is one of the things I find very challenging and may stem back to my first marriage when my husband would regularly get me to ask my parents for money when we fell short. At the time, I didn't realise that I was asking for my own money, as my parents had set up a company with my siblings and me as shareholders (together with my uncle's children). When I felt pressured to ask my parents, I experienced a deep feeling of dread in the very pit of my stomach. It is a deep fear of being judged as being incompetent. Even now, writing these words, tears are streaming down my face. I avoid this feeling.

The reflection with Tanya is the realisation that "I will be judged in writing this book." That I am "putting myself out there" ... and "who am I to write a book?" The temptation is here right now to reach for some chocolate and a hot drink rather than continue with this chapter. Reaching for food at a time of strong emotions is something I often do, rather than address the issue at hand, I will reach for something to quench this feeling of being incompetent. It could even be water, and anything will do rather than face the emotion.

For me, this also goes back to school – I remember desperately wanting to do ballet and striving to be the best. There was always one girl better than me – her name was Casey. She would always get the first prize. I could never beat her. My back was never straight enough. Little did I realise at the time that I have a heredity scoliosis (curvature of the spine). It was passed down through the paternal side of the family and generally affected the eldest daughter. As a result of this curvature, I was never going to be successful at ballet – let alone get first prize. How I wish the younger me could have understood that fact at the time, rather than be set up for the same feeling when anyone asks me for help.

This feeling of being incompetent and incapable also affects me right now, as I grapple with having to learn a new accounting program. There is a cloud-based program which has become very popular, whereas I have used a computer-based one for decades. The cloud-based one is supposedly simpler – and I feel so incompetent as I watch YouTube presentations trying to come to terms with the "new way" of accounting. The way I have responded to this need to get up to speed on the program is to procrastinate. Yes, I deliberately used those words "get up to speed" and "procrastinate." They are at odds with one another and set me up even further to be in an impossible bind. The more I try to "get up to speed," the more I procrastinate! And nothing is going to work. I have resorted to food for comfort – particularly sugary or carbohydrate-rich foods – is this anger I need to look at, possibly. All I need to do is to book onto a course and methodically go through the training. An interesting sideline is that once I wrote this down, I have been able to admit to others that "I still have my training wheels on," so can I have a little more time to achieve what needs to happen? And surprise, surprise, it's been

easy. What I need to do is to trust myself and the Universe, that I can achieve competency in the program and get done what needs to happen.

CASE STUDY

In June 2017, my dear friend Suzanne and I went for a long walk along the Warburton Trail in outer Melbourne. We were discussing various things, and I asked if I could record the conversation on my phone. The following is an edited transcript of the walk.

The trigger was betraying myself by deferring to my two travelling companions, and lying to cover the real reason/ Instead of voicing my opinion, I shut down what I really wanted to do. During the conversation, her voice changes and becomes loud with anger and frustration and rage because she listened to her head and not her heart by making sure that everyone else was happy and okay.

How often in your life have you done this? "All the time." *What does this give you?* "Not a damn thing." *Can you go deeper?* "Oh, you are so thoughtful, you are so kind." Suz realises that she gets validation for being kind and wonderful – by betraying what she wants to do. "You are so gracious. You are so compassionate, caring, thoughtful. Under this are anger and frustration because I didn't listen to myself."

Using some Journey Method™ tools, I asked her to roll the cameras back to how often in her life she had done this. *How often have you betrayed yourself to please others?* "All the time. Everything I have done, I do it to make everybody comfortable." *Check-in all the times you denied you.*

Suz became very emotional. She flashbacked. *Pinpoint a time, when was the first time you remember betraying yourself?* "There were issues around my cousins. I felt pushed to the side. I didn't stand up for myself." *Check in to see if it had anything to do with self-esteem and how you viewed you – whether you mattered, family Christmases – did you matter? How did you feel about you?* "I didn't talk. I didn't have a voice [strong emotion] I couldn't talk. I felt like I was being strangled. The decision I made was that it wasn't safe to speak up. It wasn't safe to have a voice." *How did you get validated?* "I became the fixer. I became the doer, doing things for everyone else [strong emotion]."

Suz had another strong emotion "I remember being put into a playpen and screaming and being ignored. So even screaming didn't get me what I wanted – 'Shut up, don't talk'" Suz was unable to get out what she wanted to say. "When you can't speak, the only opinion you hear is someone else's." *What's the fear?* "It's my fault." I repeated this statement about 6-8 times before she started with a litany of statements. "It's my fault for standing up to my uncle; it's my fault for not going to Christmas functions; it's my fault for breaking up the family; it's my fault I had a bad haircut; it's my fault I can't exercise; it's my fault I can't do anything right; it's my fault I can't control my emotions."

When did you decide it was "your fault?" "In my playpen. We had moved into my paternal grandmother's home for nine months, and my mother couldn't cope, she shut down. I've taken on her beliefs of not being good enough. I'm not good enough. I was standing in the cot, screaming. I take off my nappy and paint the wall with poo. I wanted to be heard. No one was listening." *When did you make that decision?* "I made it then, and I also remember being 13 – being pinned up against the classroom wall by a bully – being strangled for something I said. At that moment, I shut down. These were pivotal points."

Suzanne spoke about how she would cling to one friend, only to find that the friend's mother could complain that she was too dependent on Danielle, that she was too clingy. With three brothers, girlfriends were important. What Suzanne took on from this experience was that "I'm not good enough just the way I am."

"As a young girl, my opinion was not important. Dad negated my choices. Even now, when I don't involve Dad in decision making, he gets upset. I believed that I couldn't do anything without Dad's approval. I looked to my father for approval for validation. I needed to be a "good little girl" to get my father's approval. If I was naughty or he didn't approve of me in some way, it was 'my fault'; It was 'my fault' if my father got angry – and he wouldn't love me.

"So, when I was travelling, one of my companions represented Dad. I needed Dad's approval with all my decision making".

Suzanne had always enjoyed singing and had shut down her singing voice as well. Just after our conversation, she decided to find a singing teacher and take a tentative step in finding her voice. One of her first experiences in finding her voice came with a confrontation with her father. She arranged a coffee date with him. She wrote down all the things she had wanted to say in the past and had never had the opportunity of expressing. She asked her father to sit and listen without interrupting. She confronted her greatest fear that she would lose her father by speaking up.

The things that have changed for Suzanne during the past two years may seem small, and yet they are profound. For all of the 15 years I have known her, she had suffered monthly migraines and period pain, that has all gone. She and her husband have recently purchased a factory where he has his business – the purchase and finance went through effortlessly; she has freedom in her knees, after years of chronic issues; she is dealing with "stuff" as it arises and is able to voice her opinion gently with everyone, clearly, concisely empowered to say what it is when it is needed.

She held a fundraising night to support the work she has been doing in Nepal. She did all the work, asked for sponsorship, asked for and received donations of a variety of goods. She organised the master of ceremonies, and the line-up of artists to perform, and she raised more than $15,000. Her mum assisted in the presentation of the goods for the silent auction and was there supporting Suz all the way.

There was one person in the crowd that evening, who was extremely proud – and that was her dad. I know he was proud – because he told me. She had finally found her voice.

"Now, although this is my fourth visit, it seems like for the first time in my life, I am going to Nepal and teaching the women in the villages how to sew. I can speak clearly with the people involved and doing something I like, that I want to do. It's honouring me. Forty-five years of waking up. Enough of putting my self-esteem in someone else's hands."

There is more about Suz's journey to Nepal in the chapter on Leadership.

Why do we allow other people's words to carry so much weight? Possibly because, as children, we rely heavily on other people to make us feel good. Each of us looks outside ourselves to be validated. We get validated through a myriad of ways. We all like to be admired. Some of us like to dress up, some of us like to perform, sing, to tell jokes, some of us like to achieve through academia, some through work. Others of us are quiet achievers.

Why is it that an 18-year-old can be so affected by the words his uncle spoke that they are still affecting him as a 50-year-old? Why does he hold onto those words? What we need to recognise is that the 18-year-old was probably so shocked at the time, that he shut down because it was inappropriate for him to respond, or he felt afraid gave away his sense of himself at that moment, and the 50-year-old is still affected by it. There is still a "hook" or "trigger" affecting the 50-year-old. The benefit of The Journey Method™ is it allows us to deal with the trauma and come to a resolution so that we are no longer triggered.

One day I sat and watched an interview between Oprah and Whitney Houston. Here was one of the world's classiest women (actually two of the world's classiest women). Whitney Huston is someone deeply admired. She achieved so much in her career. Her song "Every Woman" spoke to women. She was an American "national treasure," and here she was speaking about being Mrs Bobby Brown, trying to be a "normal" person.

What did it mean to be Mrs Bobby Brown? It meant that this woman had to be "normal" – not a world-class singer; this woman

had to dim her light. She could only love Bobby Brown. Here she was speaking how she believed the rest of the world could not love her, she could only be Bobby Brown's wife; this woman could not have her thoughts and emotions; this woman had to play "second fiddle" to her husband – what he wanted, he got; what he said went; this woman lost herself – she lost her identity; she lost her self-esteem; this woman became a little girl when he was drunk and became abusive – he spat on her.

It was painful to watch and to experience how this amazing woman downplayed her own value, her beautiful voice, and her own ability to please "her man." She spoke about losing herself, trying to be pleasing him. She could not recognise her own value. She died in 2012 from accidental drowning following an overdose.

Building self-esteem

How can you build your self-esteem? First and foremost, become aware of the story you are telling yourself. This story has developed over many years. Use a journal to write down the story. Get specific about what you believe about yourself. Ask yourself, "what else do I believe?" Write down all the negative words you have heard spoken to you, which have impacted you. Start to question every one of these words.

If you can, find a photo of yourself as a small child that you truly love and see the beauty in that child. See just how magnificent that child really is. See the potential in that child. You are still that beautiful being. You are still that magnificent. The only thing which changed is that your mind started telling you a story or you heard others telling you lies, and you have believed them. Allow your soul to find the joy inside. Tap into that joy and allow that joy to shine.

You have consciously or unconsciously created the life you are currently leading. You have manifested everything the way it is right now. When would be a good time to recognise that you can manifest whatever it is you want, to change the way your life is, to make it better? You can begin to change by changing the way you speak.

Become aware of the language you are using. If you are speaking negatively – STOP – find the language which says what you really want to say positively. Look at some of the examples in the Appendix.

The following is a post from Facebook … it is one of "those" messages we are encouraged to copy and paste. While I try to avoid them, this one resonates. It has a photo of the poster. Unfortunately, there is no way to acknowledge the original author.

I've hated this woman.

I've not loved her at full capacity.

I've fed her lies and told her she wasn't good enough and have allowed others to tell her she isn't good enough.

I've allowed her to be broken

I've allowed others to treat her disrespectfully.

I've allowed her to run through brick walls and battle for others who won't even stand for her.

I couldn't stop others from abandoning her, but I've seen her stand up and be a light for the world and love others despite all that.

I have stood come by fear while she fought battles in her mind, heart, and soul.

This woman has screwed up any times as a partner, as a mother, ad as a friend because she doesn't always say and do the "right things."

She has a smart mouth, and she has secrets.

She has scars because she has a history.

Some people love this woman, some like her, and some don't care for her at all.

She has done good in her life. She has done not so good in her life.

She goes days without makeup or shaving her legs.

She doesn't get dressed up very often.

She is random and sometimes silly.

She will not pretend to be who she is not.

She is who she is.

Every mistake, failure, trial, disappointment, success, joy, and achievement has made her into who she is today.

You can love her or not … but if she loves you, she will do it with her whole heart, and she will make no apologies for who she is.

This woman is a warrior.

She's not perfect, but she has a lot of worth.
She is unstoppable.
Gracefully broken but beautifully standing.
She is LOVE
She is LIFE
She is TRANSFORMATION
She is GRACE
She is BRAVE.
And she will keep moving forward.
She is ME.

She is YOU!

CHAPTER 5

How to be a Leader Instead of a follower

♡

Our deepest fear is not that we are inadequate.
Our deepest fear is that we are powerful beyond measure.

Marianne Williamson,
A Return to Love

CHAPTER 5

How to be a Leader
Instead of a follower

Book stores are a great way to spend a few hours, particularly when you have nothing else to do. I found myself in Chatswood (a suburb of Sydney) one day, and I was browsing in the Self-Help section and picked up *A Course in Miracles*. This beautiful version was printed on bible paper … you know the wafer-thin almost transparent type. Flimsy is a word that comes to mind. I hesitated when out of nowhere a woman appeared and handed me a book and said: "You don't need that one just yet, read this!" It was Marianne Williamson's *A Return to Love*.

The purchase duly done, I took it home and read it from cover to cover that afternoon.

The quote above says it all. We are afraid of our own power. In the ensuing years, I have become even more aware of the truth of these words.

The power Williamson speaks about is not the power that comes from control. It is about accepting that each of us has an inner strength and knowing that there is "something" we have that is seemingly unattainable. It is something we "know" yet "can't put a finger on," in other words, our minds are incapable of grasping.

Despite the circumstances of our birth, and the experiences we have during childhood, it is still this "something" that enables people to lift themselves out of poverty or adversity; the "something" that people like Nelson Mandela rely upon when they are subjected to humiliation and degradation and yet are able to lift themselves up and become the leader of their country. The "something" that Mother Theresa had was a "call" from God to work and support the poor and sick of Calcutta, India.

Having a Catholic education, that word "call" or "calling" was used frequently. For me, it was only ever mentioned with reference to a vocation to be a nun. It was never about to being or doing anything else. Yet, each of us has a "call" to be "something." To do "something." It could be to be a mum, a dad, a school teacher, a nurse, a doctor, a lawyer, a bricklayer, a plumber, a beautician, a hairdresser, an actor. The list goes on and on.

Thinking back over my life, one of the most enjoyable times of my childhood were Sunday lunches. Mum would cook a roast and all the vegies, and there would be a baked apple pie with ice cream and cream or some other delicious concoction she dreamed up or found in the latest *Woman's Weekly*. Mostly the thing I enjoyed was the debates which took place both during and after the meal. We would sit for hours, mainly debating politics and world events. My brother's friends would arrive, and they would join in, sometimes it was lively, generally though everyone was able to share their point of view and we would drink tea and coffee and eat chocolates and have fun.

It was to form the basis of an interest in politics, which endures. I love sitting in front of the television on election night listening to the banter of politicians and commentators as they try to predict the outcome.

Daring to lead

I suppose it was those Sunday debates which were behind my interest when I saw an advertisement in the local newspaper about a branch of a political party being re-formed. I was already a member of the party, so I decided to attend. I wanted to get to meet people and felt this might be an opportunity. I introduced myself to a lovely lady. I can still remember her name – Dorothy. We got talking and sharing until the meeting came to order.

A temporary chairman was nominated to take charge of the meeting. Then there was a resolution passed that the branch be formed. The next item on the agenda was the election of office-bearers. The first position to be filled was that of Chairman. At this point, Dorothy turned to me and asked if she could nominate me. Totally astounded, I said YES! Before I knew it, I had the job. In turn, the next position was that of Secretary, so I returned the favour to Dorothy, and she was duly elected. The rest of the positions were then filled.

At that point, the temporary Chairman then handed the meeting over to me. Up to this point, I had NEVER chaired a public meeting, nor had I any idea of what to say or what to do. I do remember sitting in that chair, silently exclaiming, "what the hell do I do and say now?" I did get through the rest of the meeting as I continued in the position for more than ten years.

That's the thing with fear. I could have sat next to Dorothy and said, No! It would have been fear that kept me from meeting so many interesting people. Being the election campaign manager for a Deputy Prime Minister; from being influential in the wider electorate; and developing a profile that assisted in my business.

Subsequent roles in the community arrived, and I was on the committee for the local Chamber of Commerce. It was in this role that I found myself on Australia Day 1988 when my mum was trying to call me to say that my dad had been admitted to hospital.

With no mobile phones in those days, it took until I got home from the parade at 2.30 pm for me to receive the call. Rushing to them both, it didn't take long for me to ascertain that things were bad. I had never seen gangrene before, and the thought went through my head that he was about to lose his leg. There was debate between Mum and me about how he would cope etc. He went into surgery at 4.30 pm and never recovered from the coma. His life support was turned off five days later.

It took until six months after my father died to understand my "calling." He had been pivotal in my life, and I took his death very hard. I found myself in a spiral of depression. This depression was something I had never experienced before. I felt totally out of control and in a very dark place.

It was then I found myself at a support group for divorced, separated and widowed people. I thought I would find some like-minded people who understood what I was experiencing. The group had a weekend retreat, and I went along to see what it was all about. It was the start of my journey to discovering ME and ultimately to discovering what I had come to do in this lifetime.

Again in 2004, I found myself saying YES to joining the Practitioner Program for The Journey. At the time again, I had no idea how I was going to pay for it, let alone get to the events. It was just a "YES" that came out of nowhere.

This decision has brought so many people into my life. It has forged friendships that are so fulfilling and joy-filled. One of those friends is Suzanne, about whom I have already shared.

In 2013 Suzanne accomplished two main goals: the first one was a visit to Nepal. The second one she cycled the Camino de Santiago in Spain. Both of these have been significant events in her life. The first one possibly more so, than the second, because every year since then, Suz has been back to Nepal. You could say Nepal has become important, or should I say, the women of Nepal have become important in Suz's life. Suz said YES to the women of Nepal. Suz has found her "calling."

Suzanne is a beautiful professional seamstress. She makes extraordinary wedding dresses and clothing in general. On her first trip to Nepal, she visited the Seven Women Centre (www. sevenwomen.org), an organisation which was set up by a then-young 22-year-old Australian woman Stephanie Wollard to

support and empower marginalised women in Nepal. Using the old Chinese proverb, "Give the man a fish and you feed him for a day; teach him to fish, and you feed him for a lifetime" philosophy, Suzanne went to Kathmandu to teach the women to sew. Their products are then sold around the world to support the centre.

Being with fear

Six years on from that first visit, Suzanne now goes into remote villages – and I mean remote. During her most recent trip, she travelled to Kathmandu, then took a small plane to Chitwan and then onto Kawasoti, then hopped into a very old Jeep which would have, years ago, been sent to the scrapyards here in Australia. There was wire hanging out from the two front tyres which were also cracked. There were no windows, and the doors were held on by the seat belts that were unavailable for use in the back seat. The winder for the window had been removed, and the bolt for the handle butting Suz's knee for the four-and-half-hour drive. No AC! Just a fan on the dash, and when it rained, a blue tarp was put over the canopy to stop the rain coming in. Up the mountainside on a dirt road one car wide, that had only been excavated four years before; through the dark and fog with uneven ground, and all that could be seen was the cliffside. No support railings to prevent a car or truck from sliding off down into the ravine below. She took 77 kgs of materials, stud machines, templates, scissors, needles and thread (cajoling the airlines to allow the additional weight due to the humanitarian aspect of the trip). The only thing that kept her going was a mantra which she recited over and over again – which is "I'm loved, safe and protected." Suz suggests that she said it over 500 times!

Her description of the trip brought tears to my eyes. To say that she and her companion were terrified would be putting it mildly. There had been a landslide just before their visit to the village of Bulingtar, where she was to teach the women from three different villages.

Suzanne's only motive is to support the women in these villages to have access to menstrual pads. There is such a taboo around the menstrual cycle in Nepal. There is even a special name for it – chhaupadi, which forbids Hindu women and girls from participating in normal activities while menstruating as they are considered impure. In some villages, women and girls have to segregate themselves from the rest of the family and go to a menstrual hut. Young women miss more than 12 weeks of school each year because of this tradition. Also, women and girls do not have access to sanitary products we women in the West take for granted.

When Suz arrives, the women gather in a small room – about three metres square and squat on the floor. There is an interpreter, and Suzanne hands out packs of the shields and pads, needles and thread, and off they go. She teaches the women the simple art of making a shield, and then a flannelette pad. The smile on their faces as they complete the task is what motivates Suzanne. She can physically see the changes she knows will take place for these women. As soon as one village is finished, the word spreads, and more women arrive to learn.

This is true leadership. The "road" to these villages is similar to that road that needed to be excavated around the mountain. In Suzanne's case, it is also one vehicle wide – she has single-handedly raised the funds necessary to purchase the sewing machines, scissors, needles, threads, stud machines, and accessories (to keep the pad in place). She started with contacts in Kathmandu and branched out from there into more remote villages.

Before her most recent trip, Suz held a major fundraising event. It was such fun, and a joy to witness this courageous woman send out letters seeking support. To see the result in the bank account – knowing that the funds were going to empower women was particularly rewarding.

What drives Suz to get into a broken-down Jeep and go into remote villages in the mountains in Nepal is the total unconditional love and acceptance she receives when she is there. She is a petite blonde white English-speaking woman, going into a community whose only language is Nepalese. They have never seen someone like Suz. These women come up to her to touch her skin to see if it is real. She knows she brings hope to the women. She knows that she has directly changed the lives of more than 400 women. She also is aware that there have been thousands more she has indirectly helped. The only language spoken is the language of love.

Before Suz went to Nepal on this recent visit, she set up a Foundation. There was a real dilemma in even taking this step. It was like she was not allowed to step up. Again, she had the same debilitating belief as me, that she was just to be a wife and mother, and that was her role. She could not achieve anything as she compared herself to her brothers, who are successful businessmen. She has finally said YES to herself. She is finally allowing herself to achieve all the things she wants to achieve. Even naming the foundation was a challenge. Accepting that this foundation is hers has also brought with it new strength and freedom.

It has taken lots of processing and experiencing all the emotions and working through the challenging beliefs Suz had around stepping up and into this new role of leadership. She could have been a follower and support the organisation already established and been dissatisfied as she saw ways in which the work could expand even further. Instead, she said YES to herself. She is a leader and is amazing at what she does.

The women she met on this trip have already come together and planned how they could set up a workshop and make the pads for themselves and to sell to others. This is truly an example of teaching someone to "fish!" All I can say is, "WOW!"

During this trip, she and her companion experienced terror beyond terror. On a subsequent trip to country Victoria, Suz was driving on a wet gravel road when she experienced her car swerving in the mud. The tears and the terror came flooding, to the point that she had to stop and get her husband to drive. She had the foresight to give me a call so we could process the fear immediately. She immediately went back to Nepal and the feeling of being unsafe. We did a Journey "drop-through," and a "roll-

back the cameras," to the time she experienced the terror, and was able to feel that even though she felt unsafe at the time, in fact, she was safe. Her body had stored the memory of the terror, and the swerving of the car had triggered the memory. Sometimes these are called "flashbacks." They are memories that a Journey process can deal with, and heal.

Suz is using that terror as a springboard for her next visit. Yes, she will make sure that the vehicle she hires next time is a little more roadworthy, and she also recognises that sometimes landslides happen.

A leader says YES

While we were discussing her visit to Nepal, Suz and I both came to the realisation that when offered an opportunity, a follower's first reaction is to say NO, and then regret their decision when it is too late to change their mind. A leader sees the opportunity and says YES and then sets out trying to find out how to take advantage of the situation.

She just said YES! And how to implement that "yes" comes later.

Being a leader means saying YES!

Being a leader means you have to face your deepest fears. You may feel alone, and you may feel afraid, and you do whatever it is you want to do in spite of this fear because you know that this is the place of creativity and innovation. You know that it took 39 variations of a product before WD40 came into existence.

One of the acronym's for fear is False Events Appearing Real. In some respects, this may be true, and yet fear is deeper than this trivialised version. It is an emotion I experienced for a long time without even realising.

At its worst, it can be like a knot in your stomach, which completely immobilises the entire body. At its lightest, it can be mildly terrifying. Twice in my life, I have experienced the immobilising type – once when I witnessed a car burst into flames, and there was someone trapped inside (he did escape). The second time was also related to fire when the house across the road from mine burst into flames because the gas pipes had deteriorated, and the flames were drawn back into them. On these two occasions, I had to hold my stomach as I felt it was about to launch into my throat.

These were real events occurring right in front of me – not false events! The other form of fear was a false event appearing real like the fear of entering a room because of a perceived threat. It is this type of fear most people have to deal with daily. The fear of standing in front of a crowd because of the fear of being judged. It is this fear that stops joy and excitement of achieving new experiences. This is the lot of the follower – the greyness of life – the mundane – the opting for safety over success.

Being a leader means being authentic and being present. Staying out of judgment. Staying out of catastrophe, being present.

Being a leader means being vulnerable. It's about being prepared to take a risk to fail; to risk being criticised; to risk being alive. You choose yourself over choosing to "fitting in" because to fit in is painful, yet setting boundaries around what's OK and what isn't OK. If you want to understand vulnerability in Leadership, read Brené Brown's work, or listen to her YouTube or Netflix presentations and podcasts.

Being a leader means being silent in a moment of chaos; being available to your team or family members when their lives are in turmoil; being able to sit quietly while they pour out their troubles, not trying to fix or blame because blame is simply a way to discharge pain and discomfort. Just listen, being available for a hug if necessary, and if appropriate.

Being a leader means to be empathetic, to know that you are enough. When you believe you are enough, you stop the struggle and start to listen; you are kinder to you and gentle to people around you.

Being a leader means to show up and be seen. Perfectionism is a way to numb cynicism, criticism, and ridicule. It is a shield that prevents us from being seen. It comes from a concern about what people will think of me.

Being a leader means to bring about change. To bring about change in any environment, you have to be able to have the challenging talk, the difficult one – the one where you may have to lay people off, where you may have to restructure the way you do things. This can happen in personal relationships as well. To bring about change in any relationship means to have difficult conversations. To have difficult conversations, you need to be vulnerable. You need to be able to discuss the most challenging of subjects.

Being a leader means to have practised the art of listening. How do you approach life – do you see the positive or the negative? When you speak to someone, do you look for opportunities to interject your experience of the subject about which they are speaking? Or do you allow the person to tell their story and just listen?

Being a leader means to practice moments of gratitude even if you are feeling terror because to feel this vulnerable means that you are alive.

CHAPTER 6

How to be a HERO, Not a Victim

♡

A hero is an ordinary individual who
finds the strength
to persevere and endure in spite of
overwhelming obstacles.

Christopher Reeve

CHAPTER 6

How to be a HERO,
Not a Victim

As a self-awareness coach, I have experienced working with many people who come seeking help.

Playing the victim

One particular woman came to see me for some Journeywork. As part of this work, I was doing an elicitation about where she was in her life, and where she had been. She began to describe a very traumatised childhood, which was still playing out in her life even though she was in her late 50s. What became obvious was her "victim status" was providing her with some "benefits." These benefits are not always healthy. It can be a negative one, as well.

As a result of the questions, which concentrated on asking how specifically does being a victim show up, and how will your life be better when you stay open/healthy/free from being a victim? My client was able to acknowledge that she gained attention through being/playing the victim. When challenged to experience how it felt if she could get the attention she craved without the need to

be a victim, she astounded me by announcing, "I will never let go being a victim."

After some discussion on the consequences of this decision, she was adamant that this was her decision. It is the only time in my career when I have had to say to someone that there was nothing I could do to support her.

It was so clear for me, at that moment, that for this client to get well and heal she had to be willing to let go of the lifetime of the trauma she had experienced. She was so caught up in her story of being a victim – it gave her leverage, it gave her a benefit, and it was this benefit she was unwilling to release.

Why would anyone want to be a victim? For precisely this reason. We get a benefit. We get leverage. We get attention. We get validation. We get relevance. We get to tell our story. We get sympathy. We get a perverse form of love.

CASE STUDY

Robyn is a client. She is in her mid-50s, and has never married or had children. She is desperately seeking a life partner. She has tried most of her adult life for some form of attachment, and nothing seems to work. She falls in love with men and women, who are emotionally unavailable. She wants to take care of others (on the condition that they will take care of her). Of course, the more she wants to take care, the more people pull away. It is a neediness that drives everything. Underneath is a deep sense of worthlessness and unlovability.

What is interesting in Robyn's case is that the people she is attracted to are narcissistic. The odd thing with narcissists is that the very first thing which attracts the narcissist to a person is that they perceive the person to be beautiful and to have all the attributes by way of personality, intelligence and beauty that the narcissist lacks. The crazy thing is that they then set out to destroy it all – ultimately creating another victim and subservient mentality in the one they so admired.

Narcissists start out appearing to be absolutely everything you would want in a partner. They appear to be "God's Gift." They shower you with love, attention and presents, and you believe that you have met your "soulmate." They seem to have the ability to cast a spell of wonderment and love. As with all relationships, this "honeymoon" can only last a short time before the cracks start to appear, and you have to be real. Narcissists charm, then disarm. Once they have your trust, they start to control your life by placing restrictions on you while they have total freedom. They invent circumstances to give themselves the freedom they want.

They are supercritical people – they have to be superior (because they feel so inferior); they don't care about your emotions; they will appear to be very caring, kind and considerate, asking all sorts of questions in the guise of getting to know you better, when in reality it is only themselves they care about. They will ultimately use this information to undermine, belittle and destroy. They are also very controlling, tending to isolate their victim from family and friends. They do this by constantly asking, "What did you say to your mother/family? What did you tell them about me/ us?" This barrage of questioning has the consequences of making the person being questioned withdraw from family and friends, rather than face the constant questioning. Then the narcissist uses the ploy that "I'm the only one who will take care of you," "I'm the only one who understands you." Then comes the next wave of control, which is to use violence – this doesn't have to be in the form of physical attack, although mostly it is the threat of physical attack, which is worse. It can also be in the form of emotional violence. Or, in my case, emotional and financial blackmail.

It is this emotional blackmail that is so challenging to try to explain to others. It is such a manipulative tool. It sounds so strange when replayed.

Some time ago, I was researching narcissists intending to present a workshop. It was during this time I came across the story of Jane Clough, a young 26-year-old nurse who was killed by her ex-partner Jonathan Vass in Blackpool UK. Jane was stabbed 71 times because Vass didn't want her to testify against him for a series of rapes he had committed on her beginning when she was seven months pregnant, and continuing even with their young daughter was in the room. He killed her because he didn't want to go to jail. How ironic – he ended up going to jail for a minimum of 30 years. In the documentary about the murder[3] there is a short sequence of Jane playing with her father – she is the marionette, he is the puppeteer! She is doing exactly what her father wants her to do – he is "pulling the strings." Her parents said many times during the documentary, "She always did as she was told … she was the perfect daughter."

This is written not to lay blame at anyone's door. Playing games is a normal part of life, and we do have to be careful of the imprints we put on our children, as well as ourselves. Jane's Dad could not have been aware that his daughter would end up in a relationship with a man who was a narcissist, and who would manipulate and control in such a violent way. Vass was a drifter who, as a good narcissist, was good at deception, mysterious, secretive, living a lie.

---

3. Docs: *Someone's Daughter, Someone's Son*, Bancroft TV, YouTube http://bi.tyl/0661Hji.

In my opinion, narcissists are the ultimate victims. Listen to the way they talk. There is always someone else to blame for the dilemma in which they find themselves. It is always someone else who has caused the problem. They become victims to themselves and their behaviour and beliefs. They are bullies. They are possessive, jealous and mean. They zap the joy out of life and drain the very thing that drew the person to them in the first place. They use every tactic to manipulate and control. "I'll do what I want" and "You will do as I say." When challenged, they will retaliate by saying the facts have been twisted – they will spin the facts to suit themselves.

After he murdered Jane, Jonathan Vass wrote letters to Jane and her parents. In one, he wrote, "I loved Jane more than you will ever realise. I couldn't bear to see her happy with another man. Your loss is no greater than mine. I lost my girlfriend, and I will never see … [his daughter]." In the letter to Jane, he wrote, "I consider what I did to be retribution. I'm sorry for hurting and lying to you in the past. But lying to the police, I never thought you could be so low and deceptive." Vass was unable to accept that he had done anything wrong. It was Jane's fault. There was no accountability for his actions. There is always someone else to blame. The narcissist is always the wronged party – the ultimate victim.

CASE STUDY

Another of my beautiful clients is Sam. I have known Sam for more than 12 years. Sam has got herself in more emotional scrapes than just about anyone I know. She has a loving mum and dad, and a delightful teenage son who is the centre of her life. The challenge for Sam is that she desperately needs to be loved. She will meet a charming man, fall head over heels in love with him, even going to the extent of moving in with him or have him move in with her, before really finding out what he is truly like. The men she "falls for" are "bad asses." After an initial period of joy and happiness, like most relationships, tensions build. For Sam, these tensions are because she feels her needs are not being met. She can be demanding of attention to the point of excessive texting and even stalking. She is suspicious of motives when she doesn't receive the attention she demands, and the stories she creates in her mind are deserving of Pulitzer Prize. She becomes a victim of her own mind.

If you are dealing with anxiety, there is every chance you are a victim of your mind. We need our minds for everyday life. I need to remember to put the garbage out; I need to remember the things I need to do. However, our minds also play havoc in our lives.

CASE STUDY

Rhonda is a dear friend I have known for more than ten years. Two years ago, she left her marriage of 30 years. Rhonda and her sister had been adopted as babies by two loving and caring parents. Unfortunately for Rhonda, she had felt there was something wrong with her – why else would her birth mother give her up? She grew up being the good, compliant little girl, feeling petrified she would be sent back to the children's home. She had a violent and disastrous first marriage to a narcissist and had to walk away from that relationship leaving behind her three teenage sons. For all the time I have known her, this is one aspect of her life that has caused so much pain. She was denied all access to the children, and even now – 30 or more years on, her children still do not want anything to do with her. She has abandonment issues on abandonment issues. Despite numerous attempts to contact her children, they have never responded. There are now grandchildren from whom she is also estranged.

As I am writing, Rhonda's divorce from her second marriage is before the court, and she is faced with what can only be described as a "double bind." She had so many dreams for her retirement. Rhonda and her husband had purchased a caravan, and they were going to travel Australia. Up the west coast to Darwin; down the centre to Uluru and Kings Canyon and Alice Springs; and up the east coast to Cairns and back through central Queensland. This dream vanished into thin air, and Rhonda has found it difficult to let go. The bind is she chose to leave the marriage.

On the day the divorce was processed, her now ex-husband put on Facebook – "It's two years today since I became a homeless, jobless bum – still loving it, ain't finished yet." And she fell into a heap. He has moved on to a new love, and Rhonda is a mess.

She went to the doctor recently and discovered she had what was first diagnosed as a tumour in her foot. It turns out it was arthritis. She was able to do some research using Inna Segal's work from *The Secret Language of Your Body*, she discovered that a tumour is:

Holding on to anger and resentment from the past. Carrying guilt, remorse and shame. Difficulty forgiving yourself and others. Complaining about life. Worrying but not wanting to make changes. Feeling Stuck and limited.

We laughed when she said that the foot had only started to play up in the last two weeks. Surprise, surprise, her divorce was processed through the courts during this time. Her ex's new love contacted her on Messenger, and she had been invited to a wedding from his side of the family where the ex and the new love are going to attend.

All the emotions set out in Segal's book were playing out in Rhonda's life. We could even add those about the tumour – believing that nobody cares about you. Experiencing jealousy and envy towards others. Right there and then. It is the classic "victim" scenario. When we processed the emotions, she uncovered anger and rage at an abusive former husband. The rage was enormous. There was so much pain surrounding the relationship. We also took the opportunity to look at how she was exacting revenge.

Revenge is insidious. I had a belief that it was only going to affect the person with whom I was angry. This belief is so not true. Revenge has a way of affecting so many others along the way. It deeply affects us. We are consumed with "getting even." "Getting even" is just deep-seated anger.

Revenge can be overt or covert. Either way, it is still revenge.

She was able to release the emotional pain, and she reported two days later that the pain the foot had subsided, and she will check in with her doctor whether she will need surgery.

Can Rhonda successfully move on from the relationship and the tumour? Yes, she can. She has done many energy cord cuts between both the relationship and the travel. She has to do it her way. In a way she needs to heal in her own time.

Is it possible to survive a narcissist? Yes, it is. I have survived two.

Is it possible to heal from being a narcissist or a victim? I believe yes, it is.

In both cases, the very first step is to recognise the emotional abuse. Not only the emotional abuse you have perpetrated on others; most importantly, you need to recognise the emotional abuse you have perpetrated on yourself. This would have to be one of the hardest lessons I ever learned in my life. During my life, I lived on a rollercoaster of emotions even though I was unaware of it at the time. One minute I would feel loved, adored and cherished. The next, I would feel devalued, discarded and abused. Sometimes it felt like I was losing my mind. I could not understand how someone could go from being loving and caring, and the next to being so abusive. The odd thing was that I could not explain it to anyone. It was impossible to have any language which could adequately describe what I was experiencing.

The first step I took to extricate myself from both of my marriages was to admit that I was unhappy. That emotion I could describe. It was probably the only emotion I knew. In an earlier chapter, I wrote about sitting with a dictionary and typing out all the feeling words I could find in a dictionary. Google was not available at the time. I spent days ticking off the various emotions. I had to teach myself how to feel. Then I had to admit to my family that I was leaving. On both occasions, they were very supportive. I had to dig deep to discover and accept that I was loved and supported, despite being told otherwise by my husband.

The one thing I found most difficult, particularly in my first marriage was to have no contact. Reading a lot about how to break away from a narcissist, the suggestion have no contact was the most challenging, particularly as I had two children to consider. I did ultimately move to the country, and it was a financially difficult decision. With my second husband, it was much easier. I moved interstate. Removing myself from the constant threat of stalking and intimidation was a good move (pardon the pun).

The main emotions I had to face anger and fear, as well as humiliation and betrayal. Once I accepted and came to terms with them, the best tools in my emotional "toolkit" were a pen and journal.

We all have narcissistic needs – the need to feel valued, admired, understood, or recognised. There are times when we become more narcissistic. However, once we recover, we return to a baseline and become more giving in our relationships. The narcissist never returns to this equal state. They feel endlessly entitled to special consideration and attention.

I remember a situation with my ex-husband who fronted up to the Virgin counter to get on a plane, and when things didn't go his way, he knocked over the monitor of the check-in operator. He then went on to verbally abuse her when she challenged him.

He was lucky actually to be allowed to board the flight. He was totally unaware of the presence of security monitoring his every move. He felt entitled to perform and justified his stance for the next 24 hours. I felt like I wanted to crawl in a hole in abject shame and humiliation.

The narcissist finds it challenging to move past certain circumstances where what is happening to him/her is more important and more upsetting than your needs. This was particularly evident in my first marriage when my husband told me he had suffered from the mumps at the age of 18, and maybe it was because of this, I was unable to fall pregnant. It was HIS fault. I had to feel sorry for him. The mere fact that I was a woman, and this was my whole purpose in life was not allowed to come into it. It took me years of therapy to overcome.

The main feelings I began to emerge over time were frustration, fear of confrontation, exhaustion, the uncertainty of where I stood with both of these narcissists, inadequacy, neglect, disempowerment, loneliness, and alienation from family and friends.

The second step in my recovery process was emotional healing. It took me years to find the support I really needed. One aspect of the narcissist's behaviour, which I found most challenging, was their illusion of competence and control. Most of the narcissists I have been involved with know everything there is about everything. They are authorities on everything, and if you don't agree with them, you are wrong and incompetent. They have a way of belittling your knowledge and speaking with such authority that

you can't question them. They become so volatile everyone is afraid to challenge them. They also feel obliged to continually let people know how they should be doing things and correcting everyone's actions all the time. This is the main reason removing myself from the orbit of the narcissist is imperative.

The challenge we have with today's culture is that it rewards selfish and arrogant behaviour. Donald Trump and the Kardashians are exemplars where narcissism is validated and reinforced. They have become famous for being rude and insensitive. Some media celebrities are crass and obnoxious. Trump belittles and takes advantage of his role as president to the point of trying to become a dictator. The media can be held responsible for some of this as it caters to them. They create headlines, and because of the 24-hour news cycle, the media reports them. The narcissist and the media feed off each other.

How to overcome being a victim – once we have become aware, and have healed the trauma created by believing that we are victims, the final stage is stepping into our own true selves – EMPOWERMENT.

♡

EXERCISE

One morning a few years ago, at 2.30 am I reached for the book in which I was researching narcissism. This is what I wrote:

"Core Belief: If I receive anything, I MUST share it with everyone. The other side of that is that I don't want to share, so, therefore, I haven't allowed myself to receive anything large, because when I have received anything large such as my inheritance, I put into my home which my ex-husband made me put into both our names; when I received a large bonus from an employer, I put it into paying off my ex-husband's debts; when I received the settlement from him, I put the money into a deposit on the house I am now sharing with my son, daughter-in-law, and granddaughters; when I received money from my parents, it went into either buying something for my first husband, or into the house from which he benefitted.

I have ALWAYS SHARED any windfall!! This isn't just a belief; this is a RULE! I can feel this in my body, how I am reacting now. There is such relief in uncovering this. I had to share everything with my sister. (No wonder my first husband reacted when he wanted me to share information! My body is relaxing so much because of this realisation.

No wonder I have had the belief I had to give so much, no wonder I have felt so tired. I have always given, and given so much, not only of me – also of my resources. I have given till there was nothing left for me. This is the way I have felt in recent weeks – that there isn't anything left – physically, financially, emotionally. NO MORE – IT IS TIME FOR ME!! I NEED MY RESOURCES FOR ME!!"

This is empowerment. It is time for forgiveness and time to embrace the inner HERO.

CHAPTER 7

How Truth is More Powerful than Lies

♡

Beware of the web you weave when first you practice to deceive.

Henry James Hensley, my grandfather, wrote these words in my autograph book when I was about ten years old. They are taken from a poem by Walter Scott called "Marmion".

CHAPTER 7

How Truth is More Powerful than Lies

Veritas.

The motto was emblazoned on my school blazer pocket for more than ten years.

Santa Sabina College, Strathfield, NSW

If you tell the truth, you don't have to remember anything.

Attributed to Mark Twain

Truth and lies have been a significant part of my entire life, and it is only now that it becomes evident just how significant.

Although my school uniform was green, the logo was in black and white. The nun's habits (the clothes they wore) were black and white. It appeared to me during my early life that there were no shades of grey. It was the truth, or it was a lie. It was right, or it was wrong. There was a right way to do things, and there was a wrong way.

Growing up in a Catholic family, my parents believed everything the Church taught. We went to Mass on Sundays and major religious holidays. There were also other special days called "Feast Days" when we all went to Mass. We would process into the Church led by Dad, my five siblings, and I would march up the centre aisle and file into the pew with Mum bringing up the rear.

Everything in my family was done according to what the Church decreed. I remember when the birth control pill was first introduced and the turmoil it caused. The doctor wanted to prescribe it for Mum as she had already had six children (and a couple of miscarriages), and her last pregnancy with twins almost caused her (and the boys') death. She developed toxaemia (blood poisoning) and was confined to bed for most of the nine months. The conflicts, discussions, debates, and moral dilemmas this tiny pill caused were extraordinary. The local priests got involved and decreed that, because of health reasons, the pill could be prescribed. In the end, she took it because she knew if she got pregnant again, she would not be here for the rest of us. I know that every time she took one of those tablets, she felt she was betraying God.

The tenets of Catholicism are centred around the seven sacraments – Baptism, Reconciliation, Eucharist, Confirmation, Anointing of the Sick, Marriage and Holy Orders. As part of this tradition, it was expected that I would "receive" as many of the sacraments as I could.

Naturally, we were all baptised as young babies "receiving" the sacrament of baptism, which was a prerequisite for the remainder. The next one (which is now called reconciliation) – we called "confession." It occurred before receiving the eucharist (previously called holy communion). This generally happened around about age seven. Confession involved going into a cubicle where a priest sat behind a screen. There was a script we learned, which was written in the catechism – a small red book, which had all the prayers we had to learn by rote. The Lord's Prayer, the Apostles' Creed, the Hail Mary, the Glory Be, and the prayers of the rosary were all there. In the confessional, we divulged the sins we had committed since our last confession, and the priest gave us absolution – so we were forgiven, we were pure. We could receive the body and blood of Christ (holy communion) at Mass.

Going to confession each week was also a ritual – it was something we had to do at school – and it was the first place I now recall, I lied. How ironic! In the confessional, we had to say it was how many days/weeks since my last confession, and "I have … [state our sin]". The problem was that I was seven, and I was a "good girl." I didn't do anything wrong, or nothing I thought was wrong. At that time, I didn't lie.

Subsequently, if I had done anything wrong, I certainly wasn't going to admit it to the priest. I would never have admitted that I stole coins from my dad's money jar to buy lollies at the tuck shop – which, in hindsight, is about the only thing I remember doing wrong. I would have been too mortified and embarrassed and full of shame, and I felt he would most certainly have told my parents about it, in spite of his oath never to reveal the contents of the confessional. So, I "made up" a story about lying. Here I was lying about lying. The very thing we were being taught not to do was the thing that was encouraged.

It is understandable that as soon as I left school, I also stopped going to confession. I decided that if I ever felt disconnected from my heart because of some indiscretion, I would ask God/the Universe for forgiveness. During visits to historic churches and cathedral with confessional cubicles, throughout the world, I cringe, I feel physically sick.

Reflecting now on the Church's real aim (what they were trying to teach me – manifest/make happen), was to enlighten me to become aware of my personal behaviour and how it impacted me and my life with others and with God. What the Church actually manifested was the exact opposite. It encouraged bad behaviour, and in fact, the behaviour was reinforced every time I went to confession. It became a habit. The crazy thing is, I didn't even realise I was lying. I had no awareness around it.

Lying to avoid deeper emotions

Liars try to put you off the scent because they are avoiding a deeper emotion. The challenge for the person on the receiving end is that they are sent on an emotional rollercoaster.

One of my dear friends recently hypothesised – "Is it possible that lying is like sugar, the more we lie, the more we crave whatever it is we get from lying? The more it becomes the norm? Does lying switch off our moral compass?"

In an article in *Very Well Mind*, in June 2019, titled "The Negative Impacts of Sugar on the Brain," Joel Fuhrman MD, writes how "excess sugar impairs both our cognitive skills and our self-control … sugar has drug-like effects in the reward centre of the brain. Scientists have proposed that sweet foods – along with salty and fatty foods – can produce addiction-like effects in the human brain, driving the loss of self-control, overeating, and subsequent weight gain."

Is it possible that lying also has a drug-like effect on the reward centre of the brain? The 45th President of the United States is a master of the lie. (Then again, the 42nd President lied rather spectacularly as well). Lying appears to "feed" him. He uses lying (and Twitter) to bring attention to himself. It is a craving. He craves attention and will do anything he can to get it. Even when he is confronted with the evidence of lying, he can gaslight his way out of it. He is using lying as a way to manifest what he wants. It appears that the very thing he doesn't appreciate is that, because of his role as president, the American people (and the rest of the world) use him as their "moral compass" – if it is good enough for the president to do "it", then it is good enough for me.

One of the best liars is a conman (or woman). They are attentive, engaging, believable, convincing, sensitive, charismatic, charming, persistent, the white knight – the protector, showering love while portraying a false vulnerability. They have a fantastic back story (all lies) and can regale with quite detailed convoluted stories of a tortured past that consumes the conversation. Grooming takes place over time, generally months, as they are prepared to devote a great deal of time to the con. They take advantage of the vulnerability of relationships to get to know the deepest, darkest of secrets which they use to manipulate and control. They can pretend to be in therapy and to be open to elicit compassion (and the information they need). Over time, they promise the world and deliver nothing of substance.

After months of manipulation, they come in for the "kill" – and the "kill" usually is money. After they get the loot, strange things occur – such as they disappear. This disappearance can be emotional, in the way of withdrawing, or they actually physically leave. They lead double lives. They are ultimately parasites, evil, cruel and without a conscience, slippery, creating a web of lies and chaos. They have taken time to infiltrate the lives of the people they target, then leave behind a trail of destruction, broken marriages, devastated financial resources, shame, self-criticism, distraught, self-blame, depleted self-esteem, total distrust. An interesting podcast to listen to is "Who the Hell is Hamish," by Greg Bearup from the Australian Newspaper https://www.theaustralian. com.au/podcasts/podcast-who-the-hell-is-hamish. Is it possible that Hamish was also needing the "fix" that comes from lying? It certainly appears that this particular conman was addicted to lying and he developed it into a fine art. What happened for him is that he got caught. He is currently a "guest of Her Majesty" and will be in jail for a few years to come. Ultimately, it's the same for most liars. They get caught.

Another form of the con is gaslighting. To experience gaslighting is to experience psychological manipulation, which is very similar to being conned. When it happened to me, I thought I was going crazy. It began in small, subtle ways, such as being told that people didn't really care about me. When I would return from visiting with family or friends, I would be quizzed about what was said and who said it. When I say quizzed, this was the initial form; it soon took the form of interrogation. The information would then be fed back to me but in a completely different form. It was twisted and turned around. I would then have to affirm that this new version of events was what really took place. So, I was constantly being fed a new form of reality. If I didn't agree with the new form, then I was told I was lying.

Although I was mildly aware of the manipulation, I was committed to making the marriage work, and I felt trapped. The only way "out" of this cycle of alternative facts was to avoid my family – which it turns out, was the ultimate purpose of the perpetrator. He wanted control, and the only way he could control me was to separate me from my family.

This control is what gaslighters do. They want to control and dominate, and they use denial, contradiction and lying to unsettle and disrupt. They aim to change and undermine perceptions and beliefs. They want you to be dependent on them. They want control.

When I was in the middle of the turmoil of my experience, my self-esteem plunged to rock bottom. I was unaware of just how unhappy I was. I was unaware that this was all going on.

I was accused constantly of having affairs. I was even accused of giving my husband an STD (sexually transmitted disease) to the point of being taken to the STD clinic for what I can only describe as the most humiliating of physical examinations I have ever experienced. This also is another of their tactics – humiliate, belittle.

Strangely, it was this experience which galvanised me into action. It was the wake-up call I needed. I can clearly remember walking out of that clinic and making a very strong resolution that I would end my marriage. If that experience was supposed to humiliate and belittle, then it had the opposite effect. It energised something in me. It was a determination that I had to change something. I didn't know at the time just how powerful an experience it was. It has made me make changes in my life and those changes are still rippling through.

Are you able to change a con artist or a gaslighter? The short answer is NO! Is either of them able to change? First of all, they would have to have some awareness of their emotions and their behaviour and secondly, be prepared to do something about them. My experience of having worked professionally with a couple of conmen has been that they have been sent to therapy under some form of coercion by family members. When confronted with someone who is aware of their game, they will "play" along for a time in order to pacify the original premise; they will often enter into a game of "verbal chess." There is no real depth or insight into their behaviour, let alone their emotions. Ultimately, they ride off into the sunset to suss out their next target.

The one lesson I have learned from both of my marriages is that I am the only person I can change. I wish I had had the wisdom to realise that in my early 20s. It would have saved me a lot of heartache, pain and financial resources, and yet there is also a knowing that I would have had to experience something else to get the lessons I have come on earth to learn.

Each of us speak untruths. We "speak" them daily. These untruths can be in the form of lying to others or lying to ourselves.

We lie to ourselves when we deny what is really going on in our lives – whether that be with our health, our weight, our relationships.

We lie to ourselves when we drink energy drinks that are high in sugar and caffeine; we lie to ourselves when we take illicit drugs and pretend they don't affect us. We lie to ourselves when we drink too much alcohol and convince ourselves that we are safe to drive our cars. We lie to ourselves when we eat foods that are laden in unhealthy carbohydrates and sugar and try to convince ourselves that they do not affect our bodies. We lie to ourselves when we are in a toxic relationship and try to convince ourselves that "I am staying because of the kids," or "I'm staying because most of the time, things are good." We lie when we sell ourselves out – when we prostitute ourselves – and this doesn't mean sexually. I prostituted myself by selling myself out because I didn't want to be alone; I didn't think anyone would care about me, so I stayed and sold myself out, I put my home up as collateral for a business loan and overdraft which eventually blew out to three quarters of a million dollars and was left with precious little in the end. None of these situations is good for us. It diminishes our self-esteem

and our self-worth. The cost to me was my health – developing high blood pressure and having a stroke.

Lying can be seen as advantageous. We do it to feel better about ourselves. We want to look good in the eyes of others, we want to maintain great connections, and we are afraid that if we tell the truth, it will lead us to be viewed adversely. We lie because the one emotion we fear is shame. However, lying creates problems. It is mentally draining as you have to remember not only the lie, also to whom you told it. It increases the risk that others will be punished and that we will be punished. It creates anxiety. It causes stress. It causes disharmony. It threatens our self-esteem by preventing us from seeing ourselves as "good" people, and it erodes trust in society, and more importantly, it erodes trust in ourselves.

One of the stories I vividly remember as a child is the story of Pinocchio – a boy made of wood who magically came to life. When he lied, his nose became bigger, and the more lies he told, the bigger it got; it was only when he spoke the truth that it returned to its normal state.

Pamela Meyer, in her TEDx talk and book *How to Spot a Liar*, speaks about lying being a cooperative act. It only has power when someone else agrees to believe the lie. She goes on to cite many examples of corporate deception and double agents undermining democracy and causing death. Meyer says that lying is an attempt to connect to who we want to be, with who we are really. She says that we are lied to eight to 200 times a day – that we are ambivalent to the truth.

Being lied to, creates emotions

Working as a campaign manager for a senior politician, I had not expected that I would be subjected to lying. It was the first time I had ever encountered someone who was supposedly respected in the community and who held high office, blatantly lie. I worked for this person freely. I gave of my time, my energy and my resources to get him elected, and he lied directly to my face. Why was I surprised? Probably because we expect people who hold office to have some integrity. When I started piecing the jigsaw puzzle of his life together, nothing made sense. It appeared that he had lied to everyone. I was so disappointed. I remember walking into the polling booth at the next election and making a conscious choice to vote for the party and not the person. I love irony – he lost his seat. I guess he fitted the political mould, about whom the media and the advertising industry always have "spun" us a story. We have accepted that they lie. We are ambivalent about these lies – we take it for granted that these people/groups will not tell the truth. They know that we have accepted they lie, so they continue.

Why then is it that we expect our family, friends, and colleagues to tell us the truth?

While writing this book, a personal experience occurred when I planned to make a beautiful meal for the family as my son was home for a few days. I got up early as I planned to slow cook the chicken, vegetables and herbs that by the evening, the meat would be falling off the bone ready for the most delicious chicken pie. On my arrival home, expecting to salivate with the delicious aromas wafting through the house, I was greeted with a cold slow

www.JanHenderson.com.au

cooker. It had been disconnected from the powerpoint sometime during the day. Dinner wasn't happening. There were the tell-tale signs which pointed to the culprit – fruit and vegetable pulp in the bin and juicer parts all over the sink.

My anger and rage were building – yet, when I approached family members to find out what had happened, I was met with a wall of denials. How did it really feel? It felt initially frustrating, then debilitating and all-consuming. The rage deepened as I was left with absolutely nowhere to go. The stonewalling of denials caused several things. It caused a story to develop in my mind, which then took on a life of its own. It caused resentment to build in my chest which then caused separation from everyone. It caused pain in my body, and I had to be careful as I know if I don't deal with this pain, it will cause me to get sick. Growing up as the second eldest, I was not allowed to be angry – I would be sent to my room to "cool down." Unconsciously, this is what I still do. I find it really challenging to stand and speak what I am feeling. Instead, I tend to shut down and withdraw to try and process what has taken place – I go to my space – my "room."

Was there a solution? In fact, No. The culprit denied all knowledge. She walked away and left me with nothing. There was no apology forthcoming. She had already moved on to other dramas in her day. And what is left for me? First up, there was the practicality to be taken care of – no chicken pie. The family went out for dinner. I was still fuming, and, had I eaten, I would have taken all that toxicity into my body, and I could not do that to myself. As for those delicious aromas … well, they did eventuate overnight as the chicken needed to be cooked, and the pie was made for dinner the following night.

What I did need to deal with were the anger and bitterness. If I had held onto them, I would not be able to relate in a healthy way to my granddaughters.

♡

EXERCISE

1. How do you deal with feelings such as these? Begin by sitting in a chair, bringing awareness to your body, and feel where in the body you are feeling the emotion, keeping your awareness there till it passes. If the body wants to rage, I let it rage – if it wants to tremble, let it tremble, if it wants to shake, let it shake. The emotion will pass if you allow it. Stay out of the story, be with the raw emotion until it subsides.

2. Another way to resolve the anger is to walk it out. Go for a jog or a brisk walk and pound the pavement. Deliberately focus on the anger as you walk. Make it a short walk. (Staying in the story of the anger/rage tells the part of your brain involved that you are truly in danger, so it continues to feed you with stress hormones and adrenaline.) The true purpose of focussing on the raw emotion allows it to move through the body and calms down the hormones and adrenaline.

www.JanHenderson.com.au

3. Yet another alternative is to write in a journal. Find a spiral notebook and write out your anger/rage – your fear/terror. Download everything you are thinking or feeling onto the page of the book. When you are finished, rip the pages out and either shred or burn them. Please refrain from re-reading them or judging what has been written. The purpose is to download and get it out of your body. Re-reading will keep you in the story of what happened and perpetuate it.

When you have completed all this, you will find relating to the culprit with love and compassion very easy. Once you have dealt with your own emotions, it is easy to see that each of us comes from our traumas of the past – our wounds. We react from those wounds. We are all selfish. We take slights personally when they aren't meant that way. Coming from compassion leads to the possibility that the culprit can open into their own pain and deal with their own traumas and lies and learn to be compassionate to themselves.

How much easier would it have been if the culprit had "fessed-up" in the beginning?

Recognising and living your truth

Lying is all-pervasive and depletes us in a whole variety of different ways. While researching this chapter, I noticed my own behaviour. I was examining papers and presentations on lying. Some I found fascinating and thought that they expressed what I wanted to say. Having returned to university and needing to write essay assignments, I am conscious of plagiarism, which is the theft of another's work. Here I was, looking at how to change the material so it would be "my words." What happened was that I became really tired; I could no longer be present to write. I had to choose to stop and go and have a rest. It was during this rest time I became aware what was happening. If I presented the copied and altered material as my own, I would be lying. I would be lying to you; I would be lying to myself; I would be lying to my publisher. I would be a fraud. My body had reacted because what I was doing was not in alignment with my ethics and my truth. It had shut down so that I could barely hold my eyes open.

Once that realisation came, I was able to be present, and while I didn't come back to the computer immediately, I was able to feel better about myself. I realised that when I look for other opinions, it takes me away from the message I have been called upon to write. It wasn't my truth I would be presenting. It would be regurgitated work from others. It would not be fresh and new. It may be truth as far as someone else is concerned, and that's OK. It just isn't the truth from my direct experience, nor it is truth that needs to be presented here. The physical reaction of shutting down is what happened to me.

♡

EXERCISE

How does your body react when you lie? Do you withdraw? Do you lash out, reach for something (by way of alcohol, sugar, or food) to numb out? Do you project the emotion or emotions you are avoiding onto others by attacking or belittling? Do you deflect, change the discussion to something more palatable?

Skeletons in the closet

Most of us would be aware of the saying "skeletons in the closet." Is there a family on this planet that doesn't have a "skeleton?" The family secret that could never be disclosed. It has only been a couple of decades when a woman who gave birth to an "illegitimate child" was seen by society as "wanton," a "hussy." (The odd thing is that it takes two people to produce that child.) Unfortunately, the man could "get away with it," whereas the woman was literally left "holding the baby." The man could hide his lie; for the woman, this was not possible – she was left to carry the shame and humiliation and the knowledge that others would know "she had had sex," and be branded for the next nine months or even more.

One of the reasons for writing about truth and lying occurred during my second marriage when I came to understand that the only time my husband looked me in the eye was when he was blatantly lying. At other times, he would look away when we were talking. When he lied, he would look straight into my eyes. He would bore his eyes into mine and almost dare me to challenge what he was saying. I remember feeling so uncomfortable. It was disconcerting and disorienting. I would be thrown off balance. I felt that he was laying down a gauntlet, and it was a threat – "don't you dare challenge me on this." I can still experience those eyes, even as I write this. It was scary.

If you get an opportunity, watch Pamela Meyer's TEDx presentation and see the excerpt of Bill Clinton, where he lied on American television about his relationship with Monica Lewinsky. Become aware of Clinton's eyes and the malevolence in them. (Just as an aside, I have only now just looked at that word – "malevolence" and experienced the significance of it. If there was a single letter "i" added, the word would become "male violence.") Those eyes are the eyes of my ex-husband when he would lie to me. And it truly felt violent and threatening.

I remember the relief I felt when I realised that he was lying when he did this. There was a part of me that relaxed and went through the motions accepting that he was lying and that the truth lay somewhere else, and I may never find out. The strange thing was, I usually did discover the truth. For example, he was addicted to motorsport. One day a new car trailer arrived in the yard, and I asked where it came from? (The question I should have asked is

"When and where did you buy it?") He answered that he was "looking after it for a friend." I was sure this was a lie.

He should have known that I would find out the truth as I was the bookkeeper for his company, and had to account for all the expenditure. He thought he was cunning enough to hide it, withdrawing $500 here, $1000 here – while still maintaining his "normal" spending. After about $11,000 was taken out, the cash withdrawals stopped, and the trailer remained in the yard never being "returned" to its supposed owner. He did ultimately confess that it was his, and I was able to tell him that I knew the whole time. I don't think I ever told him how I knew he was lying. I wanted to keep that one "up my sleeve."

So, what was my ex-husband trying to achieve by lying? What is anyone trying to achieve by lying? The truth is, I cannot know. I can only hallucinate. Is the question my friend proposed earlier about sugar a possibility? Again, an obvious answer is that he was trying to cover up what he had done. If I were to go deeper to see what was under that, I would probably guess that he was afraid that he would not be loved. That the love he craved would be withdrawn. There is that word "crave" again. There is the possibility of getting some temporary relief in the body. *Did he achieve (manifest) what he was trying to do?* Initially, he achieved covering up his misdeed – the trailer stayed in the yard; long-term, he achieved the very thing he was afraid of – that he would not be loved and that the love he craved was withdrawn. *What did he feel?* Again, I can only guess that he would have felt shame and humiliation. I say that because, from my experience, that's what I would have been feeling.

Is there a difference between a promise and a lie?

Not much from my experience. A promise that becomes a reality is heart-warming and affirming. Joy and happiness elevate the spirit and energy levels, and there is a feeling of euphoria. It brings enthusiasm, and the serotonin in the body is palpable. It feels like the world is an amazing place in which to live.

On the other hand, a promise that never eventuates is a lie. It is debilitating, depressing, and degrading. Think of a child who is seriously ill and who has been promised a trip to Disneyland. Think of a parent who promises furniture for a newly married young couple who are on minimal wages and the expectation they will have a comfy lounge to sit on and will get to sleep in a bed instead of the fold-out mattress they are currently using. When the promises never eventuate, how do they all feel? The first word that comes to mind is betrayed. There are possibly hundreds of others – duped, conned, baited, trapped, to mention just a few.

Why do we promise things? Why do we say to children that they will be taken to Disneyland when we know that we don't have the financial resources to make the trip? Is it an off-hand remark to keep the child quiet? Is it that we want the child to feel better if they have something to which they can look forward? Is it that we want the child to like us instead of the other parent (competition between parents)? Is it to make us feel good? Is this the dose of sugar for us alone? Each of us is intrinsically narcissistic – we are selfish and self-centred.

Promises from the perspective of the recipient set up expectations, and when expectations aren't met, they cause anxiety, anger, and resentment, which are unable to be expressed because the recipient is always "holding out" waiting for the promise to be fulfilled. There is a belief set up, that "If I'm a good girl/boy, then the promise will be delivered." In the case of the young couple, the anger and resentment cause them to withdraw and to be "nice" to the promiser's face, but otherwise judgemental and nasty.

Promises from the perspective of the person making the promise – make them feel good in the moment. It is all about that moment of temporary gratification – it's the "sugar hit." Then they move on to the next moment without any awareness of the consequences of their behaviour. They will probably never remember the promise they made – and have no idea what others feel.

What about pretence? The Collins Dictionary defines pretence as "an action or claim that could mislead people into believing something which is not true." When we pretend, we are lying. We are deceiving ourselves as well as others. Pretence is just another way of living negatively.

We pretend when we present ourselves as being rich when, in fact, we are living on credit. We pretend when we buy the knock-off designer goods because the real designer handbag or shoes is way beyond our budget. We pretend we are intelligent when, in reality, we know very little. We pretend we can cook when we really don't know how to boil water, let alone an egg. We pretend when we pay someone to write a university assignment and submit it as our own work. The list goes on.

What about the saying "fake it till you can make it?" Does this mean that everyone who fakes it is lying? The "new age manifesting 'experts'" would have you pretend that you are something that you aren't. This is a form of lying? Yes, it is. Then how does someone who is shy, for instance, deal with their shyness? Have the shy person get some help with their low self-esteem and coach them in life skills – such as public speaking, so that they were able to access the beautiful innate confidence we all have so they no longer had to pretend that they were shy. I can remember the very first time I stood at the lectern to do a reading at Church. I felt for sure that the entire congregation could hear my knees knocking together through the microphone. I wanted to get off the altar as fast as I could. And I didn't let it stop me from doing the reading again the following week.

We all lie. And the one person we lie to the most is ourselves. Reflecting on TRUTH, I have to remind myself of all the times in my life I have lied. There have been some BIG lies, and some LITTLE ones as well – you know the ones we call "white" lies. They're the ones we tell ourselves when we feel we can't really tell the truth. Such as when the shop assistant asks us, "How are you today?" not expecting to get an honest answer. How many times I have said "I love you" when I didn't mean it; when I stole stationery from my employer; when I lie by omission – leaving something out.

And, what about lies of omission? When we tell partial truths. An example of a lie of omission occurred to me a few months into my first marriage when my husband told me that maybe one of the reasons I hadn't fallen pregnant (I wasn't taking contraceptives) was that he had suffered from the mumps when he was 18. Mumps causes the swelling in various organs of the body, normally in the neck (salivary glands), and sometimes in young men, it can result in the swelling of the testicles. This condition, known as orchitis, can result in sterility (the inability to produce sperm and hence father children). This "little piece of information" may not seem all that relevant, and it is information that should have been revealed before our marriage. It had the potential to have changed so many things (which was possibly why it was not discussed). When it was revealed, I had to face the fact that as a woman, I believed that my role in life was to be a wife and mother and it was devastating. It was like I had been kicked in the guts. I was unable to process this devastation as I was 20,000 kilometres away from my family and I was bound to secrecy.

The other reason I was unable to process the grief was that my husband constantly used the line, "How do you think I feel?" I could not cry; I could not speak; I could feel all the rage and anger deep down; it was just not allowed to surface. What I now understand occurred during this time, is that I lost joy. I lost the ability to feel connectedness. I lost me. All of these emotions took years and countless Journey sessions to unravel. Something very magical did emerge a few years later when we were able to adopt two beautiful boys – one of whom has produced the most adorable three daughters who are an absolute joy in my life, and the other is actively trying.

All of these lies have never left me – until now, as I confront them – bringing them into the light so they can be gone. Some are here with me now as I'm writing this. The dilemma I have – do I include this one – do I include that one? If I write about this lie, is it going to hurt others? What is the impact of telling them? The only thing I can do right now is to write from my perspective and know that I did the best I could under the circumstances at the time. Would I do things differently now? More importantly, can I forgive myself? Yes, I can, and Yes, I do forgive me.

Writing about telling the truth, I can remember one day. I must have been about 14 when my mother thought I was lying because she felt that I wasn't dressed appropriately for the occasion I was attending. (On reflection, I probably didn't have my hat and gloves on!!) She drove me to the event. I can still see me sitting in the car, and I can hear the conversation … "You aren't really going to this, are you? Where are you really going?" When I couldn't answer her – because I was telling the truth, she turned around and took me back home. I'm not sure whether she ever realised that on that occasion, I was telling the truth. I was punished for a perceived lie. I remember the bewilderment and abject helplessness I felt at the time – the dilemma that I was dammed if I did lie, and dammed if I didn't.

I can go back to my early 20s when I lied to my parents about seeing a new boyfriend (who subsequently became my first husband). They didn't want me to go out with him and tried everything they could to prevent the connection. They even bought me a car!! The conflict I experienced within myself at the time was excruciating.

Lying impacts the very fabric of our being. It is a denial of our very essence. It breaks trust and causes us to experience a myriad of emotions … shame, dread, disgust, humiliation, hatred, guilt, remorse, regret, contempt, confusion. It can cause us to be discredited, degraded, to be ostracised, disavowed, disinherited. The list goes on.

So why do we do it? I'm sure there is plenty of research available which will demonstrate why people lie. For myself, I know when I have lied, I have done so, because I want to avoid feeling shame, dread, disgust, humiliation, hatred, guilt, remorse, regret, contempt, confusion. I avoid these feelings, as they are uncomfortable, and rather than feeling uncomfortable, I will tell a lie. The odd thing is, when I lie, my body is in turmoil, and I need something to placate that turmoil – in my case, it is sugar. By admitting that I'm lying is a feeling of relief. My body physically relaxes and is at peace.

Telling the truth is a healthy way to act. It is open and honest. I remember an occasion years ago when I sold advertising for a magazine, and the wrong ad was used for a client. When he received his copy, he immediately called and was ready to "let me have it." He was completely disarmed when I admitted we had made a mistake (those weren't the words I used at the time – I'm sure you can interpret the correct ones without me writing them). He was taken aback and responded, "That wasn't what I expected you to say, I was ready to come through the phone at you." The issue was resolved, and we finished the call on a positive note.

As I sit here writing this chapter, I have become aware of a feeling of peace which is permeating my whole being. Writing about these various aspects of lying and confronting how lying has impacted my life, particularly the point at which I really began to lie, I can feel that younger me being forgiven. She was so confused and didn't have anyone to really guide her about what to do. She tried so hard to be perfect, and if it took lying to give the appearance of being perfect, then that is what she felt she had to do. How ironic it is since we are born innocently perfect.

Speaking the truth brings integrity, trust, virtue, sincerity, principles, forthrightness, reliability, ethics, morality, goodness, decency, well-being.

Speaking the truth builds character, veracity, reliability, trust, resilience, dependability.

CHAPTER 8

Why Love Conquers Hate

♡

Lord make me an instrument of your peace
Where there is hatred, let me sow love
Where there is injury, pardon
Where there is doubt, faith
Where there is despair, hope
Where there is darkness, light
And where there is sadness, joy
O divine master grant that I may
not so much seek to be consoled as to console
to be understood as to understand
To be loved as to love
For it is in giving that we receive
it is in pardoning that we are pardoned
And it's in dying that we are born to eternal life
Amen

The Prayer of St Francis

CHAPTER 8

Why Love Conquers Hate

This has to be one of THE most beautiful prayers ever spoken and written. The tenets behind it are powerful, and it can be said by anyone to invoke a sense of peace. The words can be said in a time of war, whether that war is with oneself, another person, a state, or a nation. It is a prayer that can be said each morning as we wake and start our day.

It is this prayer that Dr Wayne W Dyer used when he wrote *There is a Spiritual Solution to Every Problem* – a book to which I referred in the many spiritual crises I went through on my journey of self-healing.

One of those crises occurred when I was confronted with having to defend myself against a verbal attack that "came out of nowhere." Throughout my life, I have found it challenging to respond verbally when placed in such a situation. Lots of people are good at verbal attacks, and I have come to realise that there are equally more people who find it a challenge to defend themselves. Verbal abuse can render me a blubbering mess. It comes from the feeling that I could never defend myself as a child. There was no speaking back to my parents. I come from the era when the strap was used as a disciplinary tool.

It is only after the fact – mulling things over in my head where I play a game of "ping-pong" in my mind. You know the one – "I

should have said this" and "He would have said that" and then on and on it goes for hours and hours. I have played this game for most of my life. It is one of THE most debilitating states in which I find myself. I can spend hours going over and over the same thing.

In the instance of the crisis described, this game of ping-pong went on for 36 hours. I was so exhausted by the tirade in my head; I ended up speaking aloud to myself. "You teach this stuff, Jan, get a grip."

At the time, I was reading Dyer's book, and so picked it up and read a couple of paragraphs. I wish I could find the spot right now, as I would love to include it here. However, I do remember the context where I was trying to make the other person wrong and me right. He wrote words to the effect if I couldn't make them wrong and me right, and vice versa, what would happen?

I "played" with this concept for a few hours. It was really challenging. My mind went into overdrive. "What the ****, there is no way she is right, and I'm wrong." "I'm right, she's wrong"! "There's no way, I'm wrong, and she is right." Over and over, it went. Then eventually, it clicked in my mind. This other person has their opinion, and I have mine. We will never see things the same. Am I allowed to have my own opinion? Yes, I am. Is that OK? Is she allowed to have her opinion? Is that OK? Can I choose whether this person is in my life? Yes, I can. At that point, my mind went still. I had finally understood what my spiritual teachers had been saying all along. It is possible to still the mind.

Love

There is so much gratitude to Dr Dyer for his wisdom in this simple exercise. If bad behaviour is occurring around me, I step away. I make an active choice to put my attention elsewhere. Love means accepting that each of us has our way of responding, it may be completely different from my way, and I have to agree that their way is their way. There is no condoning. There is simply acceptance that the responsibility for changing the behaviour (or not) is with the other party. It is their responsibility.

There is one thing that has brought about more freedom, and therefore self-love in my life more than anything else; it is the acceptance of personal responsibility. Each of us is personally responsible for our own actions. This awareness removed the burden I was carrying, handed to me by my parents. "You have to take responsibility for the rest of them (meaning my siblings)." The way I heard this was that I needed to take responsibility for everyone! So I did! Even when my siblings wanted to take responsibility for themselves, I still had this "rule" by which I was living.

Some time ago, I experienced a period of resentment when I felt that I had to bail my son out with his car payments. I had worked hard to earn some money, and in one fell swoop, more than half of it was gone – just like that! I was trying to pay down some debt, and here I was back where I had started.

Instead of rejoicing that I had been able to help my son out financially – I went into resentment. That resentment grew over time. I started to tell myself a story – one part of which was that the only time he would call was when he asked for money. My only use to him was as a bank. The story went around and around in my mind – and the more it went around, the more resentment I felt. The truth is, none of it was true.

My resentment then extended to the rest of the family. I started telling myself other stories about them. I stopped contributing. I stopped doing for others, which in turn permeated every aspect of my life. I had developed amazing stories, and I lived out of them for some time. The resentment permeated the work I was doing with a colleague – I became intolerant and inflexible, more rigid. What's more, I resorted to purchasing lots of chocolate, sugar and cooked lots of unhealthy food. I gained about five kilos in weight and felt like a frump!

On reflection, I can see that I took on responsibility that was not mine. In taking on that responsibility, I hated myself because that hatred caused me to withdraw my love from everyone.

I am reminded of a conversation I had with my Mother, two weeks before she passed away.

Two things happened during the conversation. The first one was she said, "I can go now. I have done everything I came to do." I had a joke with her that she needed to find something else to accomplish. I wish I had realised, at the time, that she was fore-warning me of her death. Whether she was consciously aware of it at the time, I will never, of course, know. Since then, it has been in my awareness, that some part of us knows when our death is near. Most of us will ignore the message. (As an aside, Mum had always said she wanted to pass away in her sleep – and that is how it happened – she had a heart attack the night before, got my sister to take her to the doctor who did a blood test which ultimately confirmed the result – she went home, and I am forever grateful that I was the last one to whom she would speak – and she said she was going to have a rest – one from which she never woke.)

The second thing Mum said during our conversation was, "Can you ever forgive me for what happened at your First Communion?" It has taken me years to understand what she was really asking. In my anger (and unconsciously) as a seven-year-old, I had withdrawn my love from my mother. She had felt it the whole time. There was always a distance between us that she could never understand. I know how hard she tried over the years to breach that gap, and we never could. It still brings tears to my eyes as awareness of what I did caused her pain. I missed out on so much connection with her during my life.

That's what anger, resentment, revenge, and hatred do – they cause us to withdraw. These emotions cause so much pain and heartache to all involved. They take us away from love. They take us away from connection.

As children, we have a concept around the way love should look. "I know my Mum/Dad love me when they do 'this,'" (the "this" can be so random) and when the parent acts in an alternative way, the child then has a tantrum, and the story develops that the parent doesn't love them. (The story generally comes about when the child sees the way the parent reacts to other siblings.)

This story can set up various patterns around behaviour that can last a lifetime. One pattern can be that the child will do anything he/she can to get attention – such as playing out dramas, and/or making everything into a drama.

A few months ago, I was talking with a client. Her energy was high as she was describing how she didn't want to work with a colleague. "I don't want to work with her," Joanne repeated the statement more than three times. I asked her to reflect on what she was saying and what she was putting out into the Universe. I asked her to listen and really hear the words, "I don't want to work with her." The conversation went along the lines, "Can you hear what you are really saying?" "No, I can't." You are saying to the Universe that you no longer want to work. Is that what you really want. You are saying you no longer want the income you are receiving? "I'm not getting any income!" "Yes, you are getting income … you have a debt to pay off, so while you may not directly be getting money, you have a responsibility to pay what you owe. How are you going to do that if you don't work with this colleague until it is paid?"

The light finally went on when she heard what she was saying. By saying the words, "I don't want to work with Matilda," she was energetically putting up a wall to block any further income. With the realisation, Joanne was able to work through why she had taken on the anger that she felt was projected towards her and had clarity that the anger wasn't her anger. She could choose whether to take it on, or she could be still and realise that Matilda's anger was Matilda's. It had nothing to do with Joanne. While it may have been projected Joanne's way, it had nothing to do with her. Coming from a place of love requires constant vigilance.

There are a couple of major points in Joanne's experience:

When you react from a high energy point, there is a need to be vigilant about what you are really saying. The Universe hears the words and will act on them immediately. Even when you say something in anger – the Universe will hear you. In Joanne's case, the Universe could hear, "I don't want to work."

In another case, a friend was bemoaning that she was tired and "needed a break." She manifested a broken arm! It would have been better for her to say, "I need a rest." Or "I need a holiday."

In a manifesting circle at a retreat once, one of the participants started to say, "I want to lose all the baggage I have been carrying." (Meaning she wanted to be rid of all the emotional trauma she had been carrying all her life.) I stopped her at this point and said to her, "Do you want to lose all your bags while you are travelling home from this retreat?" "No!" she replied, somewhat startled. I then said, "Please, be specific about what sort of baggage you are saying. Can you put your intent in a better way?"

Returning to words

Become more aware of the words you are using, and the intent of those words. The unconscious mind goes with the literal use of them, not the intent. Remember how you interpreted words as a child. Remember how a person "on the spectrum" might hear your words. That is the way the unconscious mind interprets. There is an exercise - a list of sayings as an addendum. These are words and phrases we use daily, and which mean the opposite of what we really intend. Check them out and see if you can identify what it is you really saying and what you really want.

Another aspect of self-love is becoming aware of those times when we block the flow of life by shutting down – or suppressing. We can shut down in a heartbeat. Shutdown occurs when we want to cry (or be joyful), and we know that people around us will act adversely. In the past, they may have told us to "stop crying" or "don't overreact" and we are trying to "keep it together."

We shut down in order to "hold the emotion inside." The challenge with holding the emotion inside is that if we keep burying them, the more stoic we feel, and the more stoic we feel, the more toxicity is held within our body. The more resentment we feel, the more this resentment is expressed as an "edge." Mostly we have no awareness of this edge. It becomes second nature to us. It can sometimes be described as "having a chip on our shoulders."

Jealousy is like this "chip," it is similar to resentment. It is also nasty and toxic. If you are jealous, you are likely to have an edge to every communication you have with those around you. You are likely to react to the slightest comment, look or perceived slight. You are likely to react with anger, bitterness and viciousness.

CASE STUDY

My dear friend Rhonda is a great **case study on jealousy**. As a tiny baby, she was the first to be adopted by two loving and caring people. A sister came along four years later. What Rhonda didn't realise for more than 60 years was that she had been jealous of her sister for all that time. Her sister was a very demanding child because she had a physical disability (pigeon-toed), and the treatment went on for more than 18 months, so the focus was away from Rhonda. The realisation came when her husband of 30 years (from whom she was separated) met a new woman. She realised that he had moved on and that she had no further relevance in his life. Then the jealousy appeared. She stalked him and the new girlfriend on social media. She was able to find out what he was up to and where he was going. Rhonda didn't want the relationship back. However, she failed to understand that the anger and jealousy were hiding deeper emotions.

She had to go deeper to find out the real reason for the jealousy – which was a feeling of abandonment. Once she became aware of the real reason, she was able to file for divorce and experience true freedom. There is now no hook between them, and Rhonda feels free and ready to get on with the rest of her life.

The jealousy affected Rhonda throughout her life; she was constantly comparing herself – she always felt that there was something wrong with her because she didn't have what her sister had. It was the material things that came easily to the sister, whereas Rhonda had to struggle for what she achieved. Rhonda was jealous of the lifestyle her sister had, for a time. The death of her brother-in-law brought them both closer, and, fortunately, the jealousy dissipated.

Throughout this book, I have tried to focus on the positive aspects of each of the chapters, giving you a perspective of what each means. So here goes, the positive aspects of LOVE – there are no negative ones!

Love means recognising what serves you. If you find yourself in a situation where the opposite is happening, ask yourself, "What would best serve me?" On Christmas Day 2009, I asked myself this very question. The decision I made at that time took nine months to implement. It is a decision in which I have rejoiced ever since.

Love means checking every single thought you have, and asking the same question: "Does this thought support me?" If it is other than supportive, then choose whether it can stay or go.

Love means having awareness around everything you do and say. Again, if it is compassionate to you, then continue. Otherwise, you will know what you can choose.

Love means being kind and considerate to you. When you are kind and considerate to you, then you will be kind and considerate to others. It is a natural extension.

Love means being present. When you are present, when you are in the NOW, nothing else exists. To take a line from the Beatles, "All you need is LOVE!"

www.JanHenderson.com.au

EPILOGUE

When I first started writing this work, there was no awareness of the journey on which I was embarking. It has all unfolded as if by magic.

This magic is part of my life, just as it is a part of yours. All it takes to access it is to be still.

Every time I sat at my computer, and sometimes even before, I would find myself asking the question – "What needs to be included today?" I could be in the shower. I could be sitting at my table (which passes for a desk) and look out at the gumtrees, the kookaburras, the lorikeets, and the other birds as they fossick in the bushes.

In the centre of the yard is my rose garden.

One of my all-time favourite songs is "The Rose," sung by Bette Midler. Every time I listen to it, I find myself crying.

The magic of the rose bushes in my garden is a beautiful analogy for this book. The bushes were pruned when I commenced writing. They were just bare sticks – not a leaf to be found. Slowly, over time, once they had gathered the strength and nourishment they needed, their leaves began to be formed. Then the buds, and finally the beautiful blooms, appeared as spring arrived.

So too, I started with a blank canvas – or should I say a blank Word document. Slowly the words appeared, and the magic happened. Whenever an example was required, either myself, the family, a friend, or client would go through the same thing about which I was writing.

Conversations would be happening, and the realisations occur "that needs to be included."

MAGIC – **M**anifesting **A**nd **G**rowing **I**n **C**onsciousness – Your words are MAGIC – speak them consciously.

APPENDIX 1

Some examples of negative talk – and the positive alternative

Negative	Positive
At least you're not sinking	You are staying afloat
Bugger me dead	I'm astounded
Change is not something to be afraid of	Embrace the change
Could not be a more perfect day	What an amazing day
Dead easy	It's easy
Don't arrive late	Please arrive on time
Don't avoid your true feelings	Feel your true feelings
Don't be afraid	Right at this moment, are you safe?
Don't be nervous	Take a deep breath
Don't be stupid	Is there a better way?
Don't be surprised	Be aware
Don't bother me right now	Can I have some space?
Don't cross the road	Wait on the curb
Don't cry	I'm here for you
Don't drink and drive	If you want to drink, take an Uber/Cab
Don't forget / Don't ever forget	Please remember
Don't forget to update your report	Please update your report

Negative	Positive
Don't forget your bags	Remember to take your bags
Don't get out of bed	Stay in bed
Don't give up	Keep going / Stay with it
Don't leave the lights on	Turn the lights off
Don't let these deals slip away	Get these deals today
Don't listen to your negative talk	Can you say that positively?
Don't make a mess with your ice cream	Please be careful with your ice cream
Don't miss an opportunity	Make the most of your opportunities
Don't miss this one	Be there!
Don't move	Stay put
Don't panic	Stay calm
Don't park in the driveway	Please park on the street
Don't react	Stay with it
Don't run	Walk quietly / gently
Don't rush	Please take your time
Don't slam the door	Close the door gently
Don't stop	Keep going
Don't stress	Be calm / Relax
Don't struggle	Relax
Don't talk so loud	Please speak softly
Don't throw it out	Please keep it
Don't waste a minute	Please be quick
Drives me nuts	This is so frustrating
Fully sick	This is sooooo good
Good grief	I'm astounded

www.JanHenderson.com.au

Negative	Positive
He's not wrong	He's right
Hit the road	Let's go
I can't afford that	I'm conserving my funds right now
I can't begin to tell you	I'm so excited to let you know
I can't believe	I'm astounded
I can't remember	Let me think about it / That file is missing from my memory bank
I can't tell you how excited I am	I'm so excited
I can't thank you enough	Thank you so much
I can't wait	I'm looking forward to …
I cannot function efficiently if I don't get …	I really enjoy myself when …
I didn't imagine	This is amazing
I don't belong	I enjoy myself …….
I don't deserve anything good	I am open to receiving
I don't deserve to be here	I am open to being here
I don't disagree	I totally agree/I agree
I don't know	Let me think about that
I don't take everything for granted	I am open to new experiences
I don't want to leave	I want to stay
I have to fight	I'm open to finding a way around this
I hope you aren't going to work tomorrow	I hope you are staying home tomorrow
I want a break	I want to take time out/have a rest
I won't rush through my speech	I'm taking my time
I'll never get anywhere	I'm open to finding my way around

Negative	Positive
I'm a crazy lunatic	I have my challenges
I'm a failure	I'm learning new ways of doing things
I'm a loser	I'm open to exploring
I'm afraid	I'm open to finding safety
I'm an idiot	I'm open to exploring
I'm hopeless	I'm learning
I'm ignorant	I'm learning
I'm never going to give up	I'm going to keep going
I'm not complete without a man/woman/partner	I'm open to finding a new partner
I'm not creative	I create something every day
I'm not enough	I'm what I am
I'm not going hungry	I enjoy my food
I'm not interesting enough	I enjoy doing …
I'm not loved	I'm self-sufficient
I'm not messing around	I am serious
I'm not quitter	I'm a stayer
I'm not smart enough	My talents lie elsewhere
I'm running out of time	I have some issues with time
I'm stupid / That's a stupid thing to do	My talents are …
I'm weak	I'm feeling fragile
I've heard nothing but good news	Good news is all around
It doesn't feel right	This feels odd
It freaks me out	I feel scared when …
It makes me mad	I get so annoyed
It makes me sick	I feel so frustrated

Negative	Positive
It makes my blood boil	I feel so angry
It's a hard life	I'm facing some challenges right now
It's not cheap	It is a little pricey
It's not to be missed	Make sure you get to see this one
It's not uncommon to …	It's quite common to …
It's not your turn to speak	Can you please wait
It's not without cost	There is a price to pay
It's tough life	There have been challenges
It's unforgettable	It's memorable
Let me tell you honestly	*This is a sure sign you are lying!*
Never forget another password	Remember all your passwords
No worries	Okay
Not a bad idea	That's a great idea
Not a bad job	What an amazing job
Not a bad little place	Great place
Not a bad place for lunch	Great place to have lunch
Not a creative bone in my body	I have yet to find my creative streak
Not too bad	It's great
Nothing is off the table	Everything is up for discussion
Please don't give up	Please keep going
Please don't hesitate to ask	Please ask for assistance
Stop looking at your phone or you'll fall down, break your neck and everything will be a disaster	Please concentrate on the task at hand
Stop looking at your phone or you'll get hit by a car	Please concentrate on the task at hand

Negative	Positive
Stop worrying	Can you please find something positive?
They're not bad people	They are really nice people
They're not stupid	They are intelligent
Watch you don't fall down the stairs	Take care as you walk down the stairs
We couldn't agree more	We totally agree with you
What a hard life	It's been challenging
Where the hell is that	Where is that?
You can't go outside	Please stay inside
You'll never be successful	You will find your niche
You're a joke	Compared to whom?
You're a loser	Compared to whom?
You're a mistake	Compared to whom?
You're crazy	You're amazing
You're insane	You're incredible
You're not wrong	You are right

www.JanHenderson.com.au

APPENDIX 2

References

1. "What you think, and what you feel … and what manifests is always a match. Every single time. No exceptions." Esther Hicks

2. Autism is a neurodevelopmental disability that affects the way people communicate and interact with the world. Characteristics generally appear in early childhood and will be present, in some form, for life. Taken from www.amaze.org.au Shaping the future for Autism.

3. "The happiness of your life depends upon the quality of your thoughts … Take care that you entertain no notions unsuitable to virtue and reasonable nature." Marcus Aurelius

4. "You aren't allowed to be successful. You can be the power behind the throne – you can't sit on it". Moira Hensley

5. https://www.abc.net.au/news/2019-09-22/ellyse-borghi-isnt-a-rabbi-or-a-rabba-shes-a-rabbanit/11520114

6. Lipton, Bruce H. PhD. *The Biology of Belief, Unleashing the power of Consciousness, Matter and Miracles*, Updated Copyright Mountain Love Productions, 2015.

7. "Every human being is the author of his own health or disease." Buddha

8. "No matter how much it gets abused, the body can restore balance. The first rule is to stop interfering with nature." Deepak Chopra

9. "Take care how you speak to yourself – because you are listening." Centre for Pastoral Care, Virginia

10. "Our deepest fear is not that we are inadequate. Our deepest fear is that we are powerful beyond measure." Marianne Williamson, *A Return to Love*

11. 'Who the Hell is Hamish" by Greg Bearup from the Australian Newspaper https://www.theaustralian.com.au/podcasts/podcast-who-the-hell-is-hamish-4tYvlAhVE7HMBHdFwDZ8Q_AUIDSgA&biw=1454&bih=746&dpr=1.25_

12. How to tell when someone is lying. University of California – Los Angeles. (2011, May 10). How to tell when someone's lying: Psychologist helps law enforcement agencies tell truth from deception. *ScienceDaily*. Retrieved July 6, 2019 from www.sciencedaily.com/releases/2011/05/110510101627.htm_

13. "BEHAVIOR; Truth About Lies: They Tell a Lot About a Liar" By Richard A, Friedman AUG. 5, 2003 https://www.nytimes.com/2003/08/05/health/behavior-truth-about-lies-they-tell-a-lot-about-a-liar.html

14. *The Negative Impact of Sugar on the Brain* by Joel Fuhrman, MD. Medically reviewed by a board-certified physician. Updated June 09, 2019.

JAN HENDERSON

Author Profile
Self-awareness coach and mentor

Jan Henderson is a self-awareness coach and mentor who supports people in overcoming challenges to reach their full potential. Those challenges can include day-to-day anxiety, stress, depression or ill health.

She has run major retreats and presented seminars for 50–200 people in business, life and self-awareness coaching over the past 15 years.

Jan has a broad cultural understanding that enables her to relate to people from different backgrounds. She has travelled extensively throughout her life, spending time in New Zealand, Indonesia, Singapore, Japan, Hong Kong, China, India, Thailand, Fiji, USA, Canada, South Africa, Senegal, Gibraltar, Spain, Portugal, France, Italy, Luxembourg, Vatican City, Greece, Austria, Germany, Switzerland, Amsterdam, the Netherlands and the United Kingdom.

Prior to becoming a full-time coach, Jan's diverse range of experience includes running two successful federal re-election campaigns for an Australian Deputy Prime Minister, as well as running her own secretarial business.

Jan is a member of the International Institute of Complementary Therapies and a Director of Journey Outreach, a charity set up to help people in South Africa and India. She is also a director, supporter and friend of the SMD Foundation, an organisation that teaches women in remote Nepalese villages how to sew.

Jan is the author of *Speak Positively – Say What You Really Mean to Manifest What You Really Want*. She lives in a three-generational household in Melbourne, Australia with her daughter-in-law and three granddaughters.

www.JanHenderson.com.au

RECOMMENDED
RESOURCES

Bays, Brandon, *The Journey*, Atria Paperback, Division of Simon & Schuster Inc. 2012

Brown, Brené, *Dare to Lead*, Penguin Books, UK, 2018

Dyer, Wayne W. *There's a Spiritual Solution to Every Problem*, Harper Collins Publishers

Lipton, Bruce. *The Biology of Belief*, Hay House, 2015.

Fritz, Robert, *The Path of Least Resistance*, Fawett Books, NY, 1984

CORPORATE TRAINING WITH JAN

Need a dynamic speaker and trainer for your next conference?

Motivate your team, increase awareness of how they communicate and bring a positive vibe to every aspect of your business.

Jan has extensive knowledge about emotional wellbeing and how what we say impacts our lives.

For more information please contact Jan at corporate@janhenderson.com.au

MENTORING

Would you like Jan to mentor you?

One on one sessions regularly, helps you to understand how to speak more positively.

Become more aware of the language you are using. Regular mentoring sessions assist you to work through any issues you may be having in day to day life.

Spots are available for either six to 12 months mentoring programs. During this time, you will expand your self-awareness, deepen in your realisation of the impact your language has on your life.

Next step: Visit my website:

www.janhenderson.com.au and fill out the Mentoring application.

Real Change ... Real Results

www.ingramcontent.com/pod-product-compliance
Lightning Source LLC
Chambersburg PA
CBHW072006090426
42740CB00011B/2106